TREVOR PONDER

Memory Improvement

How to Boost Your Brain Power and Remember More

First published by IQ Self LLC 2023

Copyright © 2023 by Trevor Ponder

All rights reserved. No part of this publication may be reproduced, stored or transmitted in any form or by any means, electronic, mechanical, photocopying, recording, scanning, or otherwise without written permission from the publisher. It is illegal to copy this book, post it to a website, or distribute it by any other means without permission.

Trevor Ponder asserts the moral right to be identified as the author of this work.

Trevor Ponder has no responsibility for the persistence or accuracy of URLs for external or third-party Internet Websites referred to in this publication and does not guarantee that any content on such Websites is, or will remain, accurate or appropriate.

Designations used by companies to distinguish their products are often claimed as trademarks. All brand names and product names used in this book and on its cover are trade names, service marks, trademarks and registered trademarks of their respective owners. The publishers and the book are not associated with any product or vendor mentioned in this book. None of the companies referenced within the book have endorsed the book.

The information contained in this book is for general informational purposes only. It is not intended to provide legal, medical, or professional advice, nor should it be relied upon as such. The author and publisher are not liable for any actions taken or not taken based on the content of this book.

The content of this book is based on the author's research and experience and is believed to be accurate at the time of publication. However, the author and publisher make no representations or warranties, express or implied, regarding the information's accuracy, completeness, or timeliness.

This book may contain links to third-party websites or resources. These links are provided solely as a convenience to the reader, and the author and publisher are not responsible for the content, accuracy, or availability of these sites or resources.

The opinions expressed in this book are solely those of the author and do not necessarily reflect the views of the publisher or any other entity.

The reader assumes full responsibility for any actions taken or not taken based on the information contained in this book. The author and publisher disclaim all liability for any loss or damage arising from or in connection with the use of this book or any information contained herein.

This disclaimer shall be governed by and construed by the laws of the jurisdiction in which this book is published. Any disputes arising out of or in connection with this disclaimer shall be resolved by binding arbitration by the rules of the American Arbitration Association.

The reader agrees to be bound by this disclaimer by using this book.

First edition

This book was professionally typeset on Reedsy.
Find out more at reedsy.com

May this book be a guide on your journey to better memory and greater mental agility. May it inspire you to make the most of your natural talents and lead you to new frontiers of learning and understanding.

"Memory is the treasure house of the mind wherein the monuments thereof are kept and preserved."

- Thomas Fuller

Contents

Foreword

As I learned more about the fascinating world of memory improvement, I became acutely aware of the challenges we face in retaining the overwhelming amount of information we encounter. Then, I realized that memory is not a static capability but a malleable one - we can all work towards improving our memory through the right approaches and techniques.

In this book, I have shared my insights and practical strategies for memory improvement. By drawing on the latest research and providing simple exercises, I hope to offer readers clear pathways to enhance their cognitive abilities and reach their full potential for learning and retention. Be it a student, a professional, or anyone simply curious about memory improvement, the strategies and techniques outlined in this book can help maximize their mental prowess.

My ultimate hope is that this book will serve as a valuable resource to anyone looking to unleash the full potential of their mind.

Acknowledgement

I would like to extend my deepest gratitude to all those who supported me throughout the writing of this book. To my family and friends, thank you for your unwavering encouragement and belief in my abilities. To my editor and colleagues, thank you for your invaluable feedback and guidance. And to all the readers, I hope this book helps you discover the wonders of memory improvement and enriches your lifelong learning journey.

CHAPTER 1

The Power of Memory through Connection

Enhancing your memory can be done with various strategies and techniques. Creating meaningful associations between memories, reciting and repeating details to ensure they are remembered. Visualizations can all help improve the recall of past events.

Additionally, using body signals such as adrenaline and energy when practicing recall can also help, as well as taking the time to relax when feeling frustrated.

It is also beneficial to create images in mind by drawing diagrams or pictures, which can then be connected to facts and relationships to make it easier to remember specific details. Combining verbal data with abstract conceptions may also aid in recollection for more efficient information finding.

Reciting and repeating the information can be an effective way to engage your memory. To help with recall, try to find a quiet area of the room where you won't be distracted by outside noise or other people.

This will aid in improving your short-term memory as you work to remember details. Additionally, taking a stroll down memory lane can also help by stimulating the brain and aiding in the recollection and storage of memories.

Going down memory lane can be difficult at times, but there are various strategies for sharpening short-term memory. Repetition is one of the most effective methods; repeating information out loud will help recall.

Additionally, it helps to find a quiet area where you won't be distracted, and visualizations can also improve your memory.

The Three-Step Questionnaire Process

Cultivating an imagery strategy to recall details can be essential to creating long-term memories. Practicing this technique can help you make connections that are easy for your brain to access when needed.

One way to do this is by using the three-level questionnaire method, asking yourself questions such as what you can see on the object, what colors you see, and whether the item relates to something else associated with the object. This technique can help you recall details easily and effortlessly with some practice!

To help recall a moment in your life:

1. Start by sitting or lying down in a comfortable position.
2. Take slow, deep breaths until you feel you're floating, and let yourself drift back to the memory.
3. Visualize walking through the forest on a warm summer day and observe everything around you - the trees, leaves, and grass.
4. Ask yourself what you see on them, what colors are visible, and how this object reminds you of something else.

By breaking down stored information using the three-level questionnaire technique and actively looking for connections to your memory, it will be easier for you to access the details of that moment.

If you want to sharpen your memory or improve your short-term memory, there are some techniques you can practice. Short-term memory is part of your brain that holds information for a noticeably short time. Its use is storing data you don't need to recall later, such as the cost of a product in the supermarket.

The amount of time for which one can hold on to the data in their short-term memory depends upon the attentiveness of that person.

Some ways to improve your attentiveness and, as a result, your short-term memory include practicing mindfulness and meditation, focusing on one task at a time, and keeping a journal to document what you have learned each day.

The Repetition Strategy

When trying to store information in your short-term memory, repeating the data over and over is a great way to ensure that you remember it. Your short-term memory starts working when you see or hear something, and words or pictures captured by your eyes are stored here.

However, it's only possible for most people to recall from their short-term memory with strategies for bringing information into the long term, so practicing methods to do this can be very useful.

For example, if you need to remember a seven-digit phone number, such as 437-2819, practice saying it aloud repeatedly until it sticks in your mind. Breaking up the numbers individually (e.g., four, three, seven, two, eight, one, nine) also helps with memorization.

Improving your short-term memory largely comes down to practicing often. As you practice, your brain can keep the information in your short-term memory active and alive for longer. This is why memorizing a seven-digit phone number such as 437-2819 can be more difficult when it's all said together than broken up into two-digit chunks (e.g., 43, 72, 81, nine).

By breaking up the numbers into smaller groups and repeating them several times, you are giving your brain more chances to store the information for later recall. However, this doesn't just apply to memorizing phone numbers—practicing different methods can help you improve your short-term memory in any area!

Try reading the list a few times to remember items on a shopping list and then mentally picturing each item.

For example, if you need to remember to buy hair dye, chocolate syrup, jam, milk, Coke, hair gel, shoe polish, shampoo, and deodorant, mentally picture each item as you read through the list. After a few minutes, try to recall the list from memory—you should be able to remember most of the items this way.

Short-term memory can help you do everyday tasks more quickly and effectively. By associating items on a shopping list with a story or image, you can remember them better than if you looked at the list. For example, imagine dyeing your hair with chocolate syrup, washing it with milk afterward, then putting jam in your hair instead of gel!

By weaving a story for each item on your shopping list, it's easier to recall them together in the right order. Short-term memory is an important temporary tool that can help us remember phone numbers until we've called someone or completed our shopping lists quickly and accurately.

To sharpen your short-term memory, roleplaying and self-talk can be effective tools. For example, you can use roleplaying to remember exact changes.

At the same time, at the cash counter—imagine yourself counting each bill and coin. Self-talk is also helpful: talk to yourself out loud as you recall the items on your shopping list or a phone number. If you have a history of memory loss due to amnesia, perseverance and practice are key – with effort over time, chunks of your memory may come back together.

Use tactics such as roleplaying, self-talk, reciting, repeating, and visualizing to improve your short-term memory. For example, when trying to recall the name of a person you haven't seen in a while, picture yourself walking alongside the person and talking like old friends.

Recite and repeat areas of the moment you can remember and associate any relevance with the visuals. With effort over time, your short-term memory may eventually increase.

Suppose you have experienced memory loss due to a head injury, disease, death, or disorder. In that case, it is important to remember that the brain stores every touch, taste, smell, word, object, and person you experience.

Even if a rare amnesia-causing disorder affects your memory, much of the information is still retrievable. It can help to let others know when you are actively trying to recall something - they may be able to help or watch closely as you try to remember. No matter what happens, each thought will last in your memory for life unless one or both of these things occur.

The mind is incredible, and those with memory loss can recall details word for word, action for action, and thought for thought once memories are together. To better understand how the mind works, we can use the analogy of a tropical rainforest.

Imagine the forest as one complete picture; each element represents different aspects of memory - short-term memory, long-term memory, perceptions, pictures, and thoughts. As you wander through the jungle, pay attention to any smells, tastes, touches, sounds, and sights that arise.

Short-term memory stores information such as a phone number for a limited period. It must be repeated a few times and re-examined until it imprints in your mind to ensure the number is in long-term memory.

Visualize the trees of a jungle being short-term memory - all spread out - and then, with each passing moment, those trees start coming together to connect with leaves, barks, and other parts of the trees, eventually forming long-term memory. This way, you'll easily recall phone numbers without constantly checking back into the phone book.

Short-term memory is a powerful and useful tool for unlocking memories. Visualizing the tropical rainforest can help sharpen your short-term memory, as each step you take brings a new tree to the forefront, and the old one quickly passes.

When trying to recall details of memories, it's beneficial to retrace your steps. Short-term memory is like a storage compartment in the brain that only holds onto things temporarily - storing everything you see, hear, smell, touch, or taste. The more repetition you give these areas of short-term memory, the easier it will be to transfer them into long-term memory.

Memories are strange things and can be elusive and powerful when triggered by the right set of circumstances. You can use visualizations and imagery to help retrieve memories from the mind.

Associations can also play a role in recalling memories, with a person or image sparking something long forgotten. Additionally, organizing thoughts into an overarching structure may help bring those details to light that were previously hidden away.

Memories can be powerful and elusive - often hard to recall, but with the right techniques, they become more accessible. Visualizing is a great way to help jog the mind and bring memories back into focus.

When done correctly, visualizations create neural pathways that remain embedded for future recall. Start by picturing yourself in a familiar place and take in all the scene details. Observe any objects that stand out, as they may evoke a memory. Form an image of this place and associate it with events or experiences from your past, reciting them out loud until they connect with memory.

Record these details and any associations that come to mind - this will help you make sense of the memories and put them in context. Construct meaningful information around the experience and reinforce the learnings.

Making memories meaningful, using distraction techniques, creating associations between these experiences, escaping traps, taking notes, and producing interferences are all other ways to aid in producing more accurate recall of memories.

Additionally, use memories you remember to sharpen your overall memory skillset. This can also involve connecting senses, ideas, words, actions, and more together to help locate information faster when needed.

Those suffering from mental disorders such as multiple personality disorder (MPD) or post-traumatic stress disorder (PTSD) should consult their therapist before attempting any memory or visualization strategies discussed above.

Although not designed for this purpose specifically, adapting these strategies may still be useful for recalling memories for those affected by mental illness.

As you journey through the path of life, pay attention to all the objects that stand out.

Notice anything that evokes a memory - people, smells, or even thoughts - and take note of them. Start to recount these memories out loud until they become associated with larger themes or storylines, and jot down any details.

This will help contextualize the memories and create meaningful information from experience. Moving along your playground of memories is essential for sharpening your mind.

Pay attention to successes and failures, highs and lows, and even those you'd rather forget. Visualizing these memories can make them easier to recall by connecting them to something tangible. Creating associations between experiences and repeating details can bring forgotten pieces of your life back into focus. Enhancing short-term memory is also important - use distraction techniques or combined memory tactics to recall information faster and more accurately.

Suppose you suffer from mental disorders such as multiple personality disorder or post-traumatic stress disorder (PTSD).

In that case, this information is not meant as advice on how to regain control of these particular types of memory – please consult with a therapist before attempting any strategies mentioned here. Nonetheless, if you have access to any information, use it accordingly.

The key is to organize thoughts into generals and specifics, associate ideas together, and write down what comes up in thought processes - all of which will help sharpen the mind and improve one's overall recollection of past events.

Positive Thinking

Positive affirmations are one of the most effective ways to sharpen short-term memory. By repeating positive phrases such as "I can remember," you train your mind to think positively and open the possibility for better recall. It may be helpful to picture yourself in a supportive environment where everyone encourages you to remember things more efficiently.

Additionally, try and focus on the details of a situation immediately after it occurs; this will help retain key information before it slips away from memory. With these strategies, you can enhance your short-term memory capabilities and take on life with greater confidence.

Using associated memories to recover lost details and make them stick is possible. Linking one event with another can create a chain of memories that helps you solidify the original memory. Additionally, taking notes after remembering something can be beneficial. This reinforces your recall abilities by writing the details down for later reference.

Lastly, replacing negative beliefs with positive affirmations, such as "I can remember," can open the opportunity for more effective memory retention. With these strategies in mind, you should experience a greater success rate in strengthening your short-term memory.

Using Recall

Using associated memories to recover lost details and make them stick is possible. Linking one event with another can create a chain of memories that helps you solidify the original memory.

Additionally, taking notes after remembering something can be beneficial. This reinforces your recall abilities by writing the details down for later reference.

Lastly, replacing negative beliefs with positive affirmations such as "I can remember" can open up the opportunity for more effective memory retention. With these strategies in mind, you should experience a greater success rate in strengthening your short-term memory.

It can be helpful to take notes after remembering something. This reinforces your recall abilities by writing the details down for later reference.

Additionally, repeating, reciting, and rewriting the details of memory as they come along can also help to solidify the memory and make it more accessible in the future. These are just a few strategies that you can use to improve your short-term memory.

Creating associations is a great strategy for strengthening short-term memory. To create an association, you can take two unrelated ideas or events and link them together uniquely. This technique can help you to form strong memories that are easy to recall later.

It is wise to use all your senses while forming memories so that they become more vivid and easier to store in your mind. Writing notes after remembering something can also be beneficial, as this allows you to refer back to them when you need assistance remembering what happened in the past.

The Repeating & Backtracking Strategy

The repeating and backtracking strategy is a great way to improve your short-term memory. By repeating information out loud or in your head and then going back and reviewing it, you can better commit it to memory. This strategy can be especially helpful when remembering items or steps.

For example, let's say you are trying to remember a list of five items. You can start by repeating the first item out loud or in your head and then move on to the next. After you reach the fifth item, you can review the list from beginning to end. This repetition method helps commit the information to memory more quickly and effectively.

There are a few methods that can help you remember multiple pieces of information:

- Repeat the information out loud or in your head.
- Write the information down.

- Create associations between the pieces of information. For example, if you are trying to remember a list of items, try linking each item to a specific color or image.
- Organize the information into manageable chunks. For instance, if you are trying to remember a long list, break it down into smaller groups of items.
- Take a break after learning the information and then return to it later for review.

Let's say you are trying to remember five items – apples, oranges, bananas, strawberries, and pineapples. To repeat and backtrack, start by repeating the first item: 'apples.' Next, repeat the second item: 'oranges.' Follow this up with the third item: 'bananas.'

Continue until you have reached the fifth item: 'pineapples.' Finally, review the list from beginning to end: 'Apples, oranges, bananas, strawberries, and pineapples.' This repetition helps commit the information to memory more quickly and effectively.

To use the technique of repeating and backtracking:

1. Start with a list of items to remember.
2. Take the first item from this list and repeat it in your head or out loud.
3. Move on to the next item on the list and repeat it.

Do this until you reach the last item on the list, then review all the items from beginning to end. This repetition helps commit the information to memory more quickly and efficiently.

Backtracking

Backtracking is a powerful memory improvement technique that involves retracing your steps in memory, starting from the present moment and working backward in time. This method is based on the idea that focusing on specific details and memories can help improve your short-term memory. By revisiting past experiences and events, you can bring those memories to the forefront of your mind and make them easier to recall later.

The process of backtracking typically involves paying close attention to specific details and emotions associated with memory. For example, if you want to remember a particular conversation, focus on the setting, the people involved, their body language, and the tone of their voices. Doing so can create a vivid and memorable image that will be easier to recall later.

Backtracking is especially beneficial for individuals with memory impairments, such as amnesia. However, anyone can use this technique to improve their memory and recall abilities. In addition to backtracking, other strategies can help you improve your memory, including:

- Focusing your attention on the information you want to remember.
- Actively engaging with the information through repetition, recitation, and review
- Keeping a pen and paper nearby to write down important details.
- Maintaining a positive attitude and believing in your ability to improve your memory.

It's important to note that backtracking, like any other memory improvement technique, takes time and practice to be effective. It's a good idea to start small and work your way up to longer and more complex memories as you get more comfortable with the process. With time and patience, you can master backtracking and enjoy improved memory and recall abilities.

Memories are meant to be cherished forever, and it is a well-known fact that once something has impacted us, it is unlikely to be forgotten. The human brain is a repository for all our memories; we must navigate through our mind's scrapbooks to retrieve them. One effective way of improving short-term memory is through the process of backtracking.

Backtracking is the process of retracing the steps in memory to understand the complete picture of the event. It involves taking mental notes and writing down key points to help put the pieces together. By doing this, you can recall not only the event itself but also the context surrounding it. The backtracking process requires complete focus and dedication, allowing your mind to flow freely to gather as much information as possible.

Your mind is a unique and powerful entity that makes you who you are. Your thoughts, beliefs, and personality are all located within your mind, and you express them through your actions and words.

Thus, keeping your memory in top condition is important, and backtracking can help achieve this. The process involves rethinking, reciting, repeating, and role-playing to bring memories to the forefront.

Based On Experience

Short-term memories are based on experiences and powerful tools that can be used to make lasting changes in our lives. Here are some tips for improving your short-term memory:

1. Make sure you get enough sleep every night, as this helps improve mental clarity.
2. Use mnemonic devices such as rhymes or acronyms to help you remember important information.
3. Break down the large tasks into smaller sections so you can focus on one task at a time and retain the information better.

4. Practice recall exercises regularly, such as writing down what you need to remember and then trying to recall it from memory later.
5. Use visualization techniques to connect concepts.
6. Exercise your brain by regularly engaging in puzzles and other mental activities that challenge memory skills.
7. Repeat information out loud to yourself to remember it better. This technique can help you commit important details to memory more easily.

It is recommended to repeat information out loud multiple times, with at least a few minutes break in between each repetition. This will reinforce the information and help you remember it more easily.

Visualization

Visions can sharpen your short-term memory by helping you observe and form memories from visual interactions, details, and colors. Visions are also articles of imagination, fantasy, and dreams. To create visions, you can draw charts and graphics or imagine them to pull up relevant details. Furthermore, imagery is another effective tool for improving memory, as it helps you to visualize interactions through pictures or diagrams.

Using colors, details, and interactions is important to remember information best. If you are attempting to recall events from the past, try using objects associated with the memory to fill in any missing pieces.

Short-term memory can process words, numbers, sensations, tastes, smells, and more - so it's important to consider all these elements when attempting to sharpen your short-term memory. Finally, envisioning yourself in a scene is another useful tool for improving short-term memory; this will help you interact with the scene as you create or recall memories.

Visualizing yourself in a particular setting can help sharpen your short-term memory. For instance, picture yourself walking through a tropical ravine and taking in the sights and sounds of the environment around you.

Imagine what it would feel like to be standing on the other side. Ask yourself questions such as, why do I find myself here? What is special about this scene that I need to remember? Focusing on these details will help you store them in your short-term memory and make it easier for you to recall them later.

Visualizing yourself in a particular setting can help you to access memories and sharpen your short-term memory. For instance, picture yourself walking through a tropical ravine and taking in the sights and sounds of the environment around you.

Imagine what it would feel like to be standing on the other side. Ask yourself questions such as, why am I here? What is special about this scene that I need to remember? Focusing on these details will help you store them in your short-term memory and make it easier for you to recall them later.

Additionally, taking out familiar pictures and examining them closely can help jog memories and cultivate new ones.

By relaxing your mind and allowing thoughts to flow without interruption, you may be surprised at the memories that come to the surface. Writing down these thoughts as they come can also solidify them and make them easier to access in the future.

This is because visualizing allows you to see things stored in your mind, even if they are not physically present. For example, after losing someone close to us, we often turn to visualization to keep that person's memory alive.

We might look at their pictures and relive the moments when they were still with us. This visualization process can also serve as a source of healing in these difficult times.

Visualization can be either a real-life image or a detailed memory representation. To effectively utilize visualization, you need to be able to match the colors and details in the image and make connections between the memory and the present.

Visualization holds the key to unlocking the images, thoughts, feelings, and ideas stored in your mind and can help you grow and improve your memory.

By visualizing yourself in the past, you can gain a new perspective on who you used to be and how you have changed over time. For instance, I was a little troublemaker when I was young, but now that I am older, I have changed for the better. Visualizing yourself can inspire self-reflection and help you become the person you aspire to be.

Take a walk on the beach, for instance. Imagine walking along the sandy shore, feeling the hot sun and the sand between your toes. See the waves crashing on the shoreline, creating ghostly white foams, and hear the seagulls flying around you.

Observe the dolphins jumping at the end of the pier and feel the sense of freedom they bring. Ask yourself how the waves and seagulls make you feel and if you have been there before. This exercise can help you recall memories and improve your short-term memory.

Roleplaying

Roleplaying is an excellent technique for sharpening short-term memory. Through roleplay, you can become an observer of yourself and explore information from new perspectives.

To engage in roleplay, you first need to create a scenario and imagine yourself as the main character in the scene. As you move through the story, take note of details such as environment, characters present, conversations that take place, etc.

This way, you focus on the situation's specifics rather than only facts. Additionally, it's important to remember to have fun with this exercise by allowing your imagination to go wild and explore different paths and scenarios. By engaging in roleplay exercises regularly, you will find your short-term memory has improved significantly over time.

Roleplay scenes can be an effective way to access lost memories. When creating a roleplay scene, it's important to focus on the details of the situation and imagine yourself as the main character in it. Include elements such as environmental details, conversations, and feelings during the scene.

Additionally, let your imagination go wild and explore different paths and scenarios. As you engage in this exercise more frequently, you will find that it sharpens your short-term memory and helps increase clarity and confidence in decision-making.

Roleplaying is a great way to access and explore your memories and improve your short-term memory. Imagine yourself as a big television screen protagonist when engaging in roleplay.

Try to concentrate on the details, such as the environment, conversations, and feelings during the scene. Don't be afraid to allow wild imagination to enter the scene – explore different paths and scenarios.

When uncomfortable or overwhelmed by memories coming up, take deep breaths and let your mind travel naturally without interruption. This exercise will help you sharpen your short-term memory and gain better clarity in decision-making over time.

Roleplaying is a great way to access and explore your memories regarding improving your short-term memory. Start by envisioning yourself as the protagonist on a big television screen and focusing on environmental details, conversations, and feelings during the scene. Additionally, use wild imagination to explore different paths and scenarios.

Taking deep breaths when overwhelmed with memories coming up can also help you travel along this journey of self-discovery naturally. Writing down the memories, you recall during roleplay can be beneficial in constructing an entire event sooner.

As humans, we always remember everything our body accepts through input resources such as the eyes, nose, mouth, and ears. However, recalling or remembering details of your life can be difficult if you have had injuries, disorders, or certain illnesses.

This frustrates the mind, making it even harder to recall or remember. The trick in these situations is to relax the mind and allow it room to recall or remember its memories.

Sometimes we fight memories that come along, which only sets back the mind. If you want to sharpen your memory, it is always best to let the memories come to the front.

Even if the memory is a tragic response, so be it. The more you let memories come to the front, the more likely you will heal from the tragedy. There are many types of role-playing that you can use to help you sharpen your mind.

The first one I would like to talk about is the role-play scene. Look in the mirror and act like you are talking to someone who looks identical to you. This should be easy, considering that it would be you in the mirror's reflection. As you look in the mirror, a picture of the other person tells you something about the memory you are trying to recover.

During this session, be sure that you are relaxed. You want to be able to put yourself in the memory. It would help if you saw the surroundings in your memory, felt the person talking to you, smelled the aroma in the air, and heard the noises around you. These things allow you to be in that place when you remember.

Note that those with mental disorders such as multiple personality disorders, currently known as dissociative identity disorder and post-traumatic stress disorder, should avoid role-playing alone. That is if you are not prepared to face your trauma. Also, note that multiple personality disorder patients often role-play in their minds, which is sometimes dangerous.

By acting in role-play, you let all your senses take over to identify a particular memory. Role-playing is a good way to sharpen your memory. I often sit in a quiet room and think about the things that have happened throughout my life, and I find them amazing.

The brain works with so many things to create your memories and make them special, not only to you but also to the people you share them with.

If this doesn't work the first time, feel free to start the process again. The more you practice, the better your mind will get. Everyone knows that saying practice makes perfect. Well, put the same to use.

The mind is a complex puzzle that holds all the pieces of our memories. Over time, the pieces can become scattered, but we can put them back together with a little effort and sharpen our short-term memory.

Writing to Improve Memory

Writing can be a powerful tool for self-improvement. We can process, reproduce, and recall information by sharpening the mind.

This process works similarly to how a computer does – by retaining any details we learn and then being able to recall them as needed. But self-improvement is more than just memory; it's also about taking action to help us reach our goals.

By engaging in activities that make us better – learning a new skill, taking on additional challenges, or discovering something new – we can develop ourselves further and become who we want to be.

Just as a nursery holds short-term and long-term memories, so does the brain. Short-term memories are ideas, experiences, and other information that we temporarily capture and store in our minds. These memories remain active for a relatively short time before being forgotten or replaced with new memories.

Long-term memories are more permanent –typically made up of experiences that have lasting impacts on our lives and remain stored in the brain for much longer. As a result, we can recall experiences from years ago as if they happened yesterday. It's an incredible feat that computers cannot replicate. Not only can the brain save memories and data without prompting, but it can also do so with more detail than a computer.

With computers, we need to save information for us to be able to recall it later; however, this is not the case with the brain. It captures every detail of an event and stores it away for easy access when needed.

This means that when we remember something that happened years ago, we can almost relive it because all the details are still stored in our brains as if they had just happened yesterday. The capacity of our brains far exceeds what can be achieved by any computer or software program – which makes us both amazing and unique.

It's amazing how the brain can store so much information for a lifetime. Unlike computers, which require us to save data to recall it later, the brain naturally captures and saves all details of an event.

This means that we can often relive past experiences by accessing their stored memory of them. It's an incredible feat that computers cannot replicate!

To help you understand associating mechanisms, we can consider a short story. Think of a time when you misplaced your keys or another item. What did you do to find those keys or other items? Did you backtrack? Did the process work?

Did you associate something in the environment with your keys to help to find them? What was the object? Was it a purse? A keyring? What else did you associate with the keys to help you locate them?

As you can see, objects of familiarity will help you find answers to your lost memories while helping you to sharpen the mind in short-term memory. Short-term memory collects information but only keeps it for a minute.

Process of Association

One of the ways to improve memory retention is through the process of association.

The power of association is the mental process of linking two or more concepts, ideas, or objects together meaningfully. This process helps us to understand and remember information by connecting it to something we already know. The association is a fundamental human memory and learning principle and has numerous applications in our daily lives.

For example, when we learn a new word, we often associate it with a related concept, image, or experience to help us remember it. Similarly, when we learn a new fact, we may associate it with a specific event or person to help us recall it later. This process is known as a semantic association and is essential for building our knowledge and understanding of the world.

In addition to semantic association, there is also the process of episodic association, which involves linking a new experience to an existing memory. For example, when we visit a new city, we associate that city's sights, sounds, and experiences with our memories of past experiences and knowledge, which helps us remember it better.

The association can also enhance our memory skills, particularly in the short term. When we associate information with a mnemonic device, such as a rhyme, acronym, or image, we can more easily recall the information when needed. This is particularly useful for remembering lists or sequences of information, such as phone numbers, passwords, or historical events.

Overall, the power of association is a powerful tool for improving our memory and learning skills. By linking new information to existing knowledge, we can more effectively store and retrieve information, which can be an asset in personal and professional settings.

This is the conscious act of linking new information with something already known. For example, suppose you meet someone named Charlie. In that case, you can associate them with Charlie Chaplin or another person with the same name to help retain the information better. The more associations you make, the stronger the information will be embedded in your mind.

It is important to maintain a positive attitude when trying to improve memory. Negative thoughts and self-talk can impede the process and prevent success.

On the other hand, if you have a positive attitude, you will be able to learn new information and retain it better than before. Your mind is like a computer, taking in information and storing it for later use. However, the difference is that the mind does this automatically, whereas a computer requires manual input.

Taking care of your mind is crucial for improving memory. Your mind accepts inputs from various sources, such as voices, things you read, noises you hear, and thoughts you collect.

Everything you do and say goes through the mind, and it is crucial to maintain a healthy and positive environment for the mind to work effectively. Your mind is like a child in a room full of toys, and it must be cleaned up and organized for future use.

The key to sharpening short-term memory is engaging in activities that challenge the mind and maintaining a positive attitude. The association is an effective technique for improving memory retention. Taking care of the mind is critical to ensuring its effectiveness. These steps can sharpen your memory and improve your ability to retain information for longer.

Music As A Powerful Tool

Music can have a powerful impact on our memory and emotions. Research has shown that music can activate brain areas responsible for emotions, memories, and language processing. This is why music is often used in therapy to help individuals access and process difficult emotions and memories.

Music can also help memory recall, especially with mnemonic devices, such as songs with catchy tunes and lyrics. When we listen to music and sing along, we practice recall and repetition, which helps strengthen our short-term memory. This is why music is often used in education to help students remember information, such as historical dates, facts, and formulas.

In addition, music can also be a form of self-expression, allowing us to express our emotions and feelings uniquely.

When we listen to music that resonates with us, we can often relate it to memories and experiences from our own lives, which helps to reinforce the memory and create a deeper emotional connection. Music can also trigger memories and emotions, allowing you to relive past experiences and feelings.

Many people associate specific songs with significant events, such as a first dance at a wedding or a graduation ceremony. When you hear that song again, your brain can recall those memories and emotions, making the experience feel like it just happened. This is why music is often therapeutic for people dealing with trauma or difficult emotions. People can process and work through their experiences healthily and effectively by using music to access those memories and emotions. You can also use music to build new memories and positive associations.

By listening to upbeat or motivating music, you can create positive associations with your daily routine, helping to improve your mood and motivation. Whether you use it to recall memories or create new ones, music has the power to impact our lives and memories in many ways positively.

CHAPTER 2

Structuring Your Ideas

The power of the mind is a double-edged sword, capable of helping and hurting you. It all comes down to how you harness its capabilities.

Navigating the maze of your mind can be challenging, with many obstacles standing in your way. You may encounter dead-ends or reflections that only show your image. Despite these challenges, it is important to continue honing your mind.

Memories can also act as barriers, with both positive and negative experiences stored away. While it's understandable to want to forget unpleasant memories, it's also important to focus on the good memories. Your mind holds all the memories you've accumulated throughout your life; unless you have a debilitating illness or disorder, you can recall them.

Take a moment to think about all the meaningful experiences you've had. Your mind will begin playing back a film of your life as soon as you do.

Even if you suffer from a physical or mental ailment, there may still be a chance to recall your memories, although it may be difficult. Speaking with a therapist before attempting any memory recall techniques is important.

While some individuals have mastered their minds, others struggle to organize their thoughts. This can cause difficulties in school, work, relationships, and everyday life.

If you constantly forget important information, you must organize your thoughts and start writing them down. The more you practice, the better your memory will become.

Keep in mind that short-term memory is fleeting and quickly forgets information. To combat this, take a closer look at the information and actively try to remember it. Finally, when faced with a difficult memory, don't give up. Instead, work around it and continue your search to define yourself.

Storage of Short-Term Memories

The storage of short-term memories in the brain is a complex process involving multiple brain regions working together. The process starts when sensory information from the environment is processed by the sensory receptors and transmitted to the brain.

Once the information reaches the brain, it is stored temporarily in the sensory memory, where it remains for a very short period, usually a fraction of a second.

Suppose the information is important enough to be processed further. In that case, it is transferred to short-term memory, which has a limited capacity and can store information for up to a minute or so. It is thought that short-term memory is in the prefrontal cortex and the brain's temporal lobe.

Once stored in short-term memory, you can transfer it to long-term memory through rehearsal or repetition. This transfer is facilitated by releasing the neurotransmitter norepinephrine, which helps to consolidate the memory by strengthening the connections between the neurons that encode the memory.

Studies have also shown that the hippocampus, a region of the brain region forming new memories, is involved in storing short-term memories. The hippocampus plays a key role in integrating information from multiple sources and linking it to existing knowledge in long-term memory.

Overall, storing short-term memories in the brain is a complex and dynamic process involving the cooperation of multiple brain regions. The better we understand this process, the better we can develop strategies for improving memory and preventing memory decline.

A lot of information is stored in your short-term memory, such as the phone number of your favorite restaurant or the route to your favorite vacation spot. Even though these memories may not be immediately necessary or used daily, your mind keeps these details in storage for future use. It acts as a virtual phonebook and map that leads you to information and knowledge.

Your mind creates a visual representation of everything your eyes see and ears hear, which is stored in your memory. However, some individuals can only retrieve information from their short-term memory if they try to transfer it to their long-term memory.

Remembering information may take a few attempts of studying. Still, with practice, your short-term memory can be sharpened, and you can recall more.

You can boost your memory by exercising regularly it. When you plan to go to the grocery store, what's the first thing you do? Some people write down a list to follow when they arrive at the store, so they don't buy something they already have at home.

But there are times when they need to remember the list before even leaving the house. To avoid this, you must review the list several times until you can remember everything. You could also walk through each store aisle instead of relying on a list.

However, even with this method, you might still need to remember what you came for or buy something you already have. If you struggle with memory, like a survivor of amnesia, recalling details, connections, colors, and the like can be difficult.

But with practice, you can sharpen your short-term memory. Repeat and recite information to help it stick in your mind. The more you repeat, the stronger the information will become ingrained in your memory.

Remember, the memories in your mind are always there waiting to be accessed; it just takes effort to retrieve them. Keep working at it, and don't be discouraged. With time and practice, your brain's garden of memories will continue to flourish.

Repressed Memories

You have faced many traumas, dramas, actions, and letdowns in your life, and as a result, some of your memories may have been robbed. However, it's crucial not to repress these bad memories and use them to your advantage. Facing your memories head-on will allow you to grow and learn rather than being held back by repressed memories.

For example, many Vietnam survivors deal with post-traumatic stress syndrome and disorders (PTSS/PTSD) and often repress memories of the war, leading to a difficult life. However, by facing those memories, you can take control and not let them control your mind and life, just like the author, who faced their traumatic memories and now can talk about anything and move forward.

Understanding the difference between short-term and long-term memories is important, as how they help you sharpen your short-term memory.

Short-term memory quickly processes the information it sees, hears, smells, tastes, touches, etc., but it spreads and is lost quickly. It's important to focus on the details and let the long-term memory take notes To make the information last longer.

The mind is like a web of information that travels through circuits and is processed, moved, and eventually rests. Associations trigger memories, and anything can be an associating object that brings back memories.

For instance, s—for a hairbrush a loved one used can trigger memories associated with that person. While these memories can bring pain, if you face them instead of repressing them, you will also start to recall good memories.

To explore these associations further, consider interacting words and how they relate to each other and trigger your memory.

For example, the words "apple" and "tree" are associated because apples grow on trees. In contrast, "microphone" and "jack" are associated because microphones are often connected to jacks. "Serious" and "funny" may not seem associated at first.

Still, if you think about it, someone who is always serious can often be humorous. By exploring these associations, you can sharpen your memory and bring back important memories that may have been lost.

In addition to the processes mentioned earlier, several other factors contribute to the brain's storage and recall of short-term memories.

One such factor is attention. To store a memory, you must pay attention to the information. The more attention you pay to the information, the more likely it will be stored in your short-term memory. This is why it is often easier to recall information when fully engaged and focused on it.

Another important factor is rehearsal. Rehearsal is the process of repeating information repeatedly. This repetition helps to consolidate the information in your short-term memory and move it into your long-term memory. Rehearsal can be done by simply repeating the information out loud, writing it down, or even mentally reviewing it.

The environment in which you learn also plays a role in memory storage. If you associate the information with a particular location or set of circumstances, it is more likely to be remembered. For example, remember a phone number better if you learned it while sitting in a specific chair.

Finally, emotions can have a big impact on memory storage. Emotional events tend to be remembered better than neutral events, and this is because the emotional response to the event triggers the brain's release of chemicals that help consolidate memory.

All these factors work together to help you store and recall short-term memories in the brain. By understanding how these processes work, you can take steps to improve your memory and recall information more effectively.

When you think back on all your memories, you will find that there are some that you would like to forget, and then there are some that you want to carry with you for the rest of your life. As you walk down memory lane, you will find that it might get tough sometimes, bringing up memories. But it is up to you to overcome them.

On the other hand, sometimes we want to remember stuff but need help. I like to write down your memory so that, in the end, you can have the whole story. This is only for some, however, because some people despise writing.

If you write the memories down, you must look over them repeatedly so that you will be able to keep building a foundation for your memory. If you encounter obstacles along the way, it is best to remove the stumbling areas, so whatever you can use will remove those blocks.

Remembering something special to you means a lot. I often take a stroll down memory lane just for the fun of it. I love looking back at all the fun times I had with my friends in school. I also have some memories that I don't want to forget and don't want to remember.

That is weird. Let me tell you why I say this. When I was a teenager, I had a girlfriend I cared about a lot.

However, she passed away right after we broke up. Even though what time we broke up, it was a mutual agreement. I still felt bad at what time she passed away. I often found myself questioning whether it was my fault. And I knew it wasn't because I wasn't the man who pulled the trigger. But it still seemed like a bad dream, and I played a part in it.

I also knew that the reason we broke up was that she was going to college. She didn't want to promise herself to me, and she'd be hundreds of miles away. So, there was no reason. I could not remember the memories that we shared.

This story is written to see how old memories can pull up tools for sharpening the mind. You want to focus on short-term memory since short-term meditation quickly passes it. You can sharpen your short-term memory by pulling up old memories to cultivate new tools and information that helps you remember.

Other tools for sharpening the mind include repeating, writing, reciting, role-playing, reviewing, previewing, and writing. Get a sharper mind.

Memory is an important place in our minds. However, there are times when you may need clarification on whether your memory is all that great. If you find yourself doing this, it's normal since, over the years, our minds tend to get a little rusty, and it's up to us to prime it. To help, you had better understand the importance of your mind.

The memory is like a waterfall. At times, the memories flow in gentle strides. And at other times, the memories rush in fast, depending on how much water is upstream.

If you have trouble remembering things, then you are the memories that gently flow in. And suppose you have problems remembering things, and practice daily to sharpen your memory. In that case, you are the memories that rush in.

At what time memories start to come back to you, you will have the chance to shut them out or allow them in. As my suggestion, you should allow the good and bad ones in. If you shut the bad memories out, you will create a barrier, affecting how you think in the long run.

If you decide to repeat your memories, make sure that you do it alone. Or if you were going to be around other people, make sure you tell them that you were repeating to remember.

Did you know that every thought that crosses your mind lasts a lifetime? This is, of course, if you don't suffer from any disease or disorder that may affect your memory. Memory is a precious thing to have. Without it, we would be lost. Do you ever sit back and think about what we would be like without a brain? We would be useless.

Our bodies cannot function properly without a brain. Therefore, you must do everything you can to help sharpen your memory. Make sure that you try repeating to sharpen your memory. This may work better for you than any other method.

Repeating is repeatedly saying until you can remember what you have said without looking it up. Still, you can use other tactics to sharpen the memory. Music is a great way to sharpen the mind, especially if you consider tactics.

For instance, if a favorite song is playing on the radio, instead of focusing on what you like about the song, let the song drive your memories to an instant in your life.

If you notice how your memories respond, you will see the waterfall flowing rapidly down memory lane. This is just one idea; however, you can also recite information to help you recall and remember effectively.

The more you recite, the better the short-term memory will respond. If you need help learning, it is probably because your mind is not focused on the need to be more subjective.

Therefore, relaxing before starting to study can help you move the blocks that trap your mind and hinder your learning. The mind will work with you if you put forth the effort. If you try to fight the mind, it only tears you down.

Therefore, as your memories develop, form, and let you in on details, go with them by letting the water flow smoothly without fighting or interrupting the mind. The music is playing in your head as you recall that special moment in your life.

How is music related to sharpening your short-term memory? Music can take you anywhere that you want to go.

Older people use music to take them back to their childhood, the era in which they are used to listening to music. Average adults use music to take them back to their first date with their spouse. Younger adults use music to reminisce on memories they have shared with their friends.

At what time you used music to go back in time, you were sharpening your short-term memory. As you listen to the music, you can see how music has changed over the years.

Songs that may have been a hit in the 70s may be modified and be a hit today, but only in a younger version. It does not matter. However, it all depends on what music holds in store for you and your memory.

As you listen to a song, you tend to memorize it over time. The first you hear it, you know nothing about it, but you like the song's tone.

The second time that you listen to it, you begin to familiarize yourself with the words. The third time you hear the song, you can sing the song aloud with the artist.

And the fourth time you heard the song, you could sing it without the artist. Now, do you see how music can help sharpen your short-term memory?

At what time you are trying to remember something fast, you must go over it repeatedly until you have a firm grip on the subject that you are trying to remember.

For instance, you see a friend at the store that you haven't seen in a while, and you want to go and see them sometimes. Therefore, you ask her for her address. She doesn't have a piece of paper, so you must memorize it. She tells you then to repeat it back to her. Later, after you get through talking to her, you ask her to verify it again to ensure that you got it right.

However, you tell her the address this time without her telling you first. This is a good way to sharpen your short-term memory.

To sharpen your short-term memory, you must practice. Do you know the saying practice makes perfect? However, the statement is not false. We are all flawed. Repeating is a great instrument for sharpening memory. However, you can repeat too much and forget what you learned.

In other words, moderation is the ideal tool for any area of life to enhance any situation, including memory. Other tactics work well too. For instance, you could preview or review the information you read to sharpen your short-term memory.

Tactics work wonders for sharpening the mind, and visual aids also promote memory. If you have difficulty recalling information, you can use visual aids, including music, to help you remember what it is you want to remember.

Memories are always in mind. No matter what you do in life, everything you learn, hear, smell, and so on is in your mind. The mind is like a tunnel; in each area of the tunnel, information is waiting for you to associate it with new information.

Thus, associating objects, words, et cetera, can help you sharpen your memory. Go ahead and walk through that tunnel using visual aids, music, previewing, reviewing, and so on. Remember, the longer you look at that information, the better the odds you will remember also. Ready to backtrack again?

Backtracking again to help sharpen your short-term memory. Live today like there is no tomorrow. You have heard this saying so many times that it sometimes makes you sick. However, some still think there will always be a tomorrow, and there's not. It would be best if you took off everything that you need, day by day.

Do not leave any loose ends. Make sure you tell the ones you love that you love them, and make sure that you don't say anything that you don't mean. Because there may come a time when you don't get a chance to say I am sorry, or I love you. As the years have gone by, we Americans have learned to live for the future, not the past.

However, everything that has happened in the past that affected us can happen again. The terrorist attacks, the bird flu pandemic, and the wars that have happened in the past can all occur again.

We as a nation must look back on our memories of those events and move forward with our lives, knowing that we now know more than we did then.

At what time it comes to each of us, however, we must backtrack to sharpen our short-term memory. We never want to forget the things that have happened that left and affected our life.

If it is worth remembering, we should have the common courtesy to keep it as a memory. Your memory makes you who you are—still, those who try to see that the mind doesn't forget anything. Therefore, use the backtracker approach to face your memories.

During a lecture, sometimes we lose track of the theme because we need help understanding something in the middle and are shy to ask for clarification. This way, we understand some parts and need help understanding some. This causes a break in concentration, and thus we lose interest in that subject.

Therefore, it's always easier to ask questions to maintain a rhythm in the study. The remaining portion is easy to understand if your doubt is clarified.

Also, sometimes during the lecture, we understand what is being said, but suddenly, a question pops up in our mind: what if some factor was changed or the like? Always feel comfortable asking such doubts.

All these questions go a long way to clearing your doubts and thus maintaining your interest in the subject. The more interested you are, the easier it is to understand and remember the subject.

Keeping a notebook or a scribbling pad while listening to a seminar or presentation is always helpful. You can note down and write the important points, the points that you don't agree with, the points you want the speaker to clarify, or any such thing.

You'll realize that when raising the points that you wrote down, you remembered most of them. This happens because while you are writing down those points, they are subconsciously absorbed by your brain.

So, listen to every conversation with utmost concentration, and keep the following points in mind. Following the abovementioned points, you'll always take advantage of everything in a conversation or speech.

Removing Those Mental Blocks

There are so many occasions when we try to remember something and cannot recollect it. For example, you met somebody a few days back at the supermarket and chatted with them.

Nevertheless, today you see them walking across the street, and you cannot recall their names. However, his name suddenly strikes you as soon as you are engaged in other work.

This is the magic of our subconscious mind, and it keeps searching for your queries, even when you think you have given up. There are certain reasons why we cannot remember these things, and a better understanding of these will help you go a long way to improving your memory.

Step One. One of the factors is anxiety. Whenever there is an important or urgent matter to investigate, something will go missing, like when everyone's ready to go to the party. Inadvertently the keys of the car will go missing, or your dad will misplace your glasses. This is normal and not to be blamed on your memory.

Step Two. Another reason for diminished memory may be depression. We get depressed when we are not feeling well or mourning the death of someone close to us. Accept it as a fact that under such feelings, the mind is unable to perform to the best of its ability and will recover as soon as you start recovering from depression.

Step Three. So often we get out of the house in a hurry and need to remember some important document or something else we need to take. In such a case, once you discover that it is missing, you must retrace your steps and get back home to collect it.

This leads to much wasted time and causes much tension. The best way to get out of such a situation is by doing your work systematically or by writing down the list of things to carry on a scratchpad and checking them before you leave. It will save you time and give you peace of mind.

Step Four. Today's life is so fast-paced that we do not have the time to understand what is going on around us, and knowingly or unknowingly, we often pick up an argument that should never have taken place. Anger, rage, stress, tension, pain, and other feelings cause memory loss and blur the mind for those moments.

One must always try to maintain one's cool to avoid memory loss. You will observe that once you are out of such situations, your memory automatically returns to normal.

Step Five. Another reason why we often need clarification or remember some piece of information is due to a factor that can be called ambiguity. We meet many people daily, some of whom may share a common name.

In addition, most of us would need clarification if we were to meet four guys named Jason at the same party.

You must create a distinguished image of each of them to remember them. In addition, most European languages are so common that it is obvious that if you are learning more than one, you will need to catch up sometimes. Therefore, it is always better to go one at a time.

Step Six. The so-called sleep busters, like caffeine, tobacco, or various available pharmacy drugs, do nothing more than keep your eyes awake and let your mind sleep. How efficiently would you be able to do a task if you were asked to do it while in a deep sleep? The case with your mind is also the same.

It needs adequate rest to work properly and store the day's information. All these things make your brain work at just a fraction of the true efficiency. It is the case with other drugs like marijuana and alcohol. Although all these things initially make you feel alert, with time, they become a habit and start degrading your brain cells.

If all these stress and sleep busters are used in a restricted amount, it is fine. But an overdose of all these will lead to lifelong effects on your mind. Drinking a cup or two of coffee is normal to eliminate drowsiness, but not 10.

Strategies For Effective Learning

If we observe the people near our friends or us, we will observe that some of them are better than us in some ways, and others are not. However, what distinguishes those from us who are better at remembering data? They follow simple rules, which are stated below.

They may be following one or more of these or something else equally effective. Try to implement the following in your everyday life and see the difference. The steps are simple and ideal for sharpening the mind.

Step One. Study for shorter durations rather than a longer single sitting. When you go to a gymnasium, your body demands some rest after every half an hour or so of exercise, depending on your stamina. Similarly, your brain also needs some rest, like your body, after rigorous mental exercise to rejuvenate itself and get ready for the next session.

It would be much better to study for three sessions of two hours each rather than sit continuously for six hours at a stretch. This kind of distributed study is more effective for learning.

Step Two. Do you eat the entire day's food requirement of your body in the morning? No. At least normal people like you, and I don't. Similarly, break up your portions of study into smaller chunks. If a chapter has five different sub-topics, try doing it one at a time.

Do one sub-topic, relax for five minutes, and then revise for another 5-10 minutes to check to see if you remember everything. And then move over to the next topic and follow the same procedure. This helps in placing the material of study firmly into your brain.

Step Three. Speak out the material you must remember loudly. This way, you will know precisely how much you know and what you need to concentrate on. After reading the material once or twice, check how much has been absorbed into your mind.

Step Four. We must find some relevance in the work we are doing. You can ask yourself some questions like, why am I doing this? Or will it do any good to me, or anybody else for that matter?

Try to associate what you were learning with your past or someone you know. This way, it becomes more personal, and you can remember it easily because it now relates directly to you.

Step Five. It would help if you concentrated as much as possible when studying and learning something difficult. Shut out all the distractions like music, or turn your cell phone on to silent mode. Try to avoid answering the doorbell or the phone. Avoiding such distractions helps one to concentrate better on the task.

Step Six. What happens when we draw a line on a piece of paper? It makes a visible mark. However, what happens when you draw another superimposing line on it? It becomes darker. The more the number of times you draw the line, the darker it becomes.

Similarly, when you repeat a certain material you learned, it imprints on your brain. The more the number of times you repeat it, the more firmly it is imprinted on your mind. Not only does repetition help you to create a strong imprint, but it also increases your confidence in the subject. Finally, the darker the imprint, the lesser the time for retrieval. Ready for some tactics?

Reciting. Say aloud that you will not have recourse to recidivism. Say, I will not recourse or relapse into the state of mind that will hinder my process of sharpening my memory. Say aloud that you will stop telling yourself that you can't remember and start telling yourself that you can remember.

Observation is the acceptable tactic of all tactics employed to help you sharpen the mind. Researchers and others interested in observation have proven that observation is one of the ultimate strategies to sharpen the mind.

I grew up using observation as my guide to survive. Unfortunately, my parents had little value in education. And the only time we went to school was when the parents felt they would get in trouble. Furthermore, I was not permitted to be in the house while my mother cooked. Therefore, I needed a teacher.

Still, I learned to cook by observation. I love potato salad and slaw, so I carefully observed the ingredients of bowls where other people cooked and went home and prepared the slaw and potato salad myself.

From observing, I cooked some of the best potato salads, macaroni salads, and slaw of anyone around. Yet the point is that our observing sharpens the mind.

If you are studying, the best idea is to study in shorter spans.

If you sit for hours at a desk, it will soon frustrate the mind. Like exercise, if you overexert yourself, you will work out without getting satisfactory results. However, as you study, observe the details you read, which will help sharpen your mind and prepare you for tests.

Taking Notes

Another great idea while studying is taking notes, which will help you back-track and review what you learned. Reviewing, previewing, and practicing are always good; this great strategy will help sharpen your mind. Previewing should be the first step since you review statements, work, and other details before you jump into it.

Observation

Observation is noting facts that come your way. The facts will help you construct a memory that will have evidence. The mind works in mysterious ways. However, you can be someone other than an expert to understand how the mind works.

Therefore, what you observe goes inside the mind and stays there. It takes you to cultivate the mind to recall and remember without problems. We can consider the following details to help you see how observation leads you to use other tactics to sharpen the mind.

Wherever you are now, single out something around you to observe. As you capture the picture in your mind, notice what follows. It would help if you were previewing, i.e., studying what you are observing without dwelling on the observation.

Before your eyes meet whatever you are looking at, preview before you note the object. Next, consider reviewing the observation as you listen to your mind to see what it is capturing. Reviewing is closely examining the observation.

Reviewing is a critical process that helps stimulate the mind and sharpens the mind at the same time. Review is the process of restudying what you studied in the first place.

Moving along, think of repeating by singling out the observation again.

Consider what you see this time as you look at the object. What is your mind saying now? What does your mind see? Could you write it down? As you notice details of the object, write down what you observe. Review the information and see what you produce.

You could next move into role-playing the scene, particularly if the object is movie-making material. In other words, act out what comes from your mind. See where it takes you. As you move along, write down what comes from your mind. Keep going. Ready to preview?

Previewing

Previewing is the process of glancing over something before you probe into it. Previewing will help you get more out of what you are doing. If you preview each time, study, take on a writing task, and so on, you will be ahead of the game every time.

Still, it would help if you considered other tactics to help sharpen the mind. Some best tactics include observation, preview, review, reciting, repeating, role play, self-talk, and facing your memories.

Most times, we forget since the mind is overwhelmed. A person can suffer anxiety, which affects the mind negatively. This often causes a person to forget things they may want to remember.

Therefore, clearing up stress by reducing stressors is a surefire way to sharpen the mind. As you move the stressors out of the way, you will notice your mind clear up.

This makes room for remembering and recalling. The mind is a trap. People set up traps in their minds. The traps sometimes include blocking memories unacceptable to the person at the time. As you block memories, you only hinder the mind's sharpening.

The mind must move freely, without reservations. Otherwise, it will fall into a pattern. We are the trainers of our minds. Everything we say, do, feel, touch, smell, hear, see, and the like goes into the mind. Once in your mind, it will remain for your life.

Unless you experience a head injury that causes memory loss, a disease of the mind, or death, everything you learned is in your mind. With this in mind, you can now preview your mind to see what is inside.

As you preview, do not be afraid, as some things make you feel uneasy. Let the thoughts go since letting them go will help you to heal from the bad memory. This is the process of developing a healthy mind and sharpening short-term memory.

Let's practice a few times to see if it can enhance your memories. Before we start, I wanted to bring up that reconstructing the mind is a great memory enhancer.

Reconstructing is building the mind. I combine role-playing and reconstruction with building my mind, and I am amazed at the results. Some people may need help finding this. However, as a survivor of lifelong amnesia, I learned that two strategies combined work wonders. Now we can practice.

Picture a memory. While the memory comes to the front, try not to dwell on the memory. Rather let the mind relax. As you move along, you will start to construct an entire scene. You can use visual aids, visualization, and other strategies to help develop that memory.

Let us practice some more. This time we are going to use associations to form a memory. Pick an object in the room. What does that object recall?

Is the object important to you? When did the object spark a memory? Keep thinking. As you continue, you will begin forming memories while sharpening the mind.

Again, before you select the object or start the process of practicing to enhance the mind, preview. Previewing is the first step to all steps in sharpening the mind. Once you accumulate your memories, start reviewing the details.

As you review, note any key areas of the memory by considering details of the memory, interactions, and colors. As humans, we see three different colors that form multiple colors, and the colors are green, red, and gray. Ready to reconstruct the mind and how to sharpen those short-term memories?

Reconstructing the Mind

Here is a list of ten names and preview each of them, read them and then say them aloud.

Megan, Maggie, Sherry, Nikki, Candy, Chrissy, Paris, Krista, Lacy, and Brandy.

Again, Megan, Maggie, Sherry, Nikki, Candy, Chrissy, Paris, Krista, Lacy, and Brandy.

Again, preview, read, read aloud, review, and stop looking at the list of names to see how many you come up with. If you get all ten names down, you are off to a good start sharpening your memory.

Next list.

Sara, Monica, Jennifer, Penny, Amber, Miss K, Michael, Mel, Jerome, Jacqueline.

Again, Sara, Monica, Jennifer, Penny, Amber, Miss K, Michael, Mel, Jerome, and Jacqueline.

Now follow the same steps you did to remember the first series of names.

After you master all ten names, rename all 20 by previewing again, reviewing, and saying the names aloud. If you follow the steps, you are reconstructing your mind, sharpening your short-term memory, and preparing to remember.

You will have no problem naming all 20 names if you do things right.

Reconstructing the mind is the process of strengthening the mind. You can also use role play to have fun and build memory as you reconstruct the mind. Let us give it a whirl. Picture yourself in a room with figurative characters you have made up in your mind.

Sit in a comfortable area of the room and carry on a conversation with these people as you draw from previous memories. You can also jump track and conjure up memories that never existed, which will associate good memories. It's ironic. However, it does wonders to sharpen the mind.

Do you have those 20 names down pat and sounding aloud as we close? Are you ready to get some effective learning to sharpen that mind of yours?

Inspiration

To sharpen short-term memory, you will need inspiration first. If you are not inspired to sharpen your mind, you will likely start and never finish the tasks. Therefore, rear up those brain cells and put those muscles to work.

If you are not inspired to sharpen your mind, read the new funny pages instead of reading this. At the same time, inspiration is a need, and other tactics or tools that we can consider while sharpening short-term memory.

Now that you have inspiration, you will also need the ability to use tools. The tools include preview and have meaning to what you learned. The tools include review, reciting, repeating, visualization, visions, senses, imagery, self-talk, role play, reconstructing the mind, building blocks, trap removal, and so forth.

We can start with this list since some of the tools for sharpening short-term memory listed work wonders. Starting with preview, we know that previewing is doing something before handling the original task. Previewing helps you to get a handle on what you are about to learn, and this helps you to move into the actual learning process without confusion.

Therefore, if you are studying for a test, preview the information before beginning to study. Rushing in only leads to memory relapses.

Still, before you start, you want to add meaning to your tasks. It is an inspirational tool since you will likely fail if there is no meaning or purpose. Reviewing is conducted after reading or learning. Once you read and learn information, you should review the information critically while making checklists to consider details too specific.

Inspiration is when we often feel like something is familiar, even if we have never experienced it. It can be so powerful that it leads us to believe in reincarnation. This feeling - sometimes called the "flash of inspiration" - comes from previous memories and experiences, even if we have no recollection!

For example, a lawyer might suddenly have a solution to an unexpected legal issue during a trial, or a surgeon could unexpectedly succeed during a delicate operation. In cases like these, the answer comes from previous learning and experiences stored in the person's mind.

This will help you get more out of reading and learning.

Reciting is speaking aloud, while repeating is restating what you heard, read, et cetera. For instance, repeating is like paraphrasing, yet at what time you paraphrase, you give brief specifics to confirm your understanding.

Repeating the information gives you the advantage of absorbing what you heard and read into the mind. This is a process of sharpening short-term memory.

Role play combined with reconstructing the mind works wonders to enhance memory. However, you want to be careful since too much can lead to stress. Try to section out the time you will role-play and reconstruct building the mind.

This will help you get more out of the visions, imagery, visualizations, repeat, review, and all the other combined tools to sharpen the short-term mind.

The processes listed overall are building blocks. Still, you want to remove traps such as battling memories, stress, overloading learning, and so forth.

Removing the traps will clear the mind so that it can perform freely. If the mind is crowded, it is like a busy subway station in New York, i.e., the interferences will distract the memory flow, which halts the mind from sharpening memory.

Let the memories go. Even if you have bad memories, let them rush since repressing memories only leads to confusion, frustration, and stress. Learning is a great tool to sharpen short-term memory.

CHAPTER 3

The Body & Mind Connection

All around us are people of all types. Some people have mastered their minds by sharpening their short-term memory. These people have moved traps out of the way and stressors from their life and use tactics to enhance memory.

Still, some people are struggling to sharpen their minds. These people have not mastered the mind and have taken control of their lives. It can happen regardless of what anyone thinks. The mind is like a hurricane. Hurricanes and gushes of wind represent storming memories. Hurricanes can sweep away obstacles, houses, et cetera, just as the mind can sweep the memories.

The only difference is that a hurricane can destroy objects, while the memory stores information learned forever. Still, if the mind suffers disease or death, it too can destroy memories and information learned. What it takes to sharpen the mind is removing traps, traps of stressors, anxiety, nervousness, distracting thoughts, and the like.

Once you remove these traps, you have cleared up memory to flow freely. Now you can download new information to bring those old memories to life. To study effectively, you will need to shorten your time studying. In other words, instead of reading for hours, say five or six, break down the study time. Learning more in less time, say around two hours is possible.

The body and mind work if you plan wisely. In other words, if you go to the gym for exercise and work out for seven hours, believing you will lose weight, you will be depressed about the overall results. Proper exercise breaks down workouts.

The body can handle working out three times per week at one-hour intervals. Likewise, the mind can work effectively if you use moderation to study. The mind needs fun and relaxation time; otherwise, you will set up traps. Rigorous exercise leaves room for traps. Therefore, take study time wisely by breaking down the workload.

The best time to study is when the body and mind are relaxed.

You should only study if you have eaten a meal. This is another trap. Since the body craves its necessities, it feeds off the mind. Therefore, you are harming two valuable parts of you that prevent you from sharpening the mind.

Let us preview. Per se, you have four chapters of information to study by tomorrow's class hour. You are now feeling uneasy and afraid you will miss out. You set up this trap in your mind. Take a few deep breaths, release a few more deep breaths, release, and tell yourself that you can do this.

Now find a comfortable area in the room, relax, and take a few more deep breaths. Say again. I can do this. If you tell yourself that you cannot, you are only building traps and will likely not finish studying.

Now preview the information you were studying by looking at each chapter. Look at the headers, topic, first sentences, and details between the pages. Study the pictures as you preview.

What you are doing now is preparing the mind for the task. Okay, now you are ready to study the first chapter. Read it slowly so that you grasp the meaning.

Have your purpose in place as you move along. Say aloud. "My purpose is to study these assigned chapters to prepare for an upcoming test. I aim to complete this task before I arrive at class tomorrow morning."

Read the chapter slowly, and after finishing, review the information. Paraphrase areas where you have questions to make room for clarification. You can recite and repeat confusing areas to help you study effectively while sharpening your mind.

Previewing is the process of preparing. Previews, for instance, are sneak previews of an entire scene. For instance, as you watch commercials on television presenting new and upcoming movies, you get a preview. This tells you immediately if the movie is something you want to watch or leave alone.

Unfortunately, studying doesn't permit you the option of deciding if you want to read or not. Therefore, preview your information first before probing into the learning process. After you preview the information, you will need to probe into the study. You are sharpening the mind to learn and grow rather than recall memories.

Either way, you can use the strategies to go in any direction you choose.

To help you prepare for previewing, we can consider a list of states and a trapper. Alabama, Alaska, Arkansas, Colorado, California, Connecticut, Delaware, Denver, Florida, Georgia, Hawaii, Illinois, and Indiana.

Preview the list. You will notice that all but one from the list is states, while the other is a city in Colorado. After reviewing the list, probe into studying the list so that you become acquainted with the order in which the list is written.

After reading the list, please review it so it registers in short-term memory. Repeat the list, recite the list, review the list again, and cover the list to see if you can recite the list entirely in order. You are starting with Alabama right down the list by reciting the alphabet. You will notice the states and cities listed in this order.

As you continue following the steps and sharpen your short-term memory, you will soon recite each state in the U.S. without a problem. Practice is essential, as well as preparing to learn. If you clear up that blizzard in your mind, you will have plenty of room to learn, grow and sharpen the mind.

Try doing the same with the following list and gradually work to name each state and city listed in this.

Kansas, Kentucky, Louisiana, Louisville, Maine, Missouri, Mississippi, and Montana.

Coordination

Coordination gives us the ability to organize our thoughts. Coordination is harmony with functioning minds that leads to effective outcomes. As you can see, organizing and coordinating the mind to work in harmony with your goal is the ultimate step in sharpening the mind.

Once you collect and gather, your thoughts will help you study, work, play, sleep, and the like much easier. Coordinating the mind and organizing thoughts will also help you reduce stressors, which is one of the ultimate reasons the mind misplaces memories.

After your thoughts are organized, and your mind is in harmony with your goals, you can take the next steps in sharpening your short-term memory.

The short-term mind is sometimes known as the vigorous or prime mind. This needs to be clarified since the short-term memory processes information at limits and stores it at the same limited processes, i.e., the memory holds information briefly.

Long-term memory, on the other hand, stores information arriving until the time indefinitely. The short-term mind stores brief information through the processes known as sensory inputting.

While the long-term collects the information, stores it, and retains it from the processes known as mental capturing. As you can see, the mind functions like a computer, i.e., information sent to a processor is stored in memory for a short time. Once the data is processed, sent to the Random-Access memory, and stored on the hard drive, it remains time.

Suppose a virus, Trojan, worm, hacker, or other dangerous contamination affects this data. In that case, the data is lost, moved, or displaced. Now that you have a brief understanding of short-term and long-term memory, how it works, and what affects the mind, you can move into sharpening the memory.

Once the memory is coordinated and organized, you can now find meaning. Meaning is a purpose intended to start and finish a task. In other words, you will need to feel your purpose and know your meaning while preparing to sharpen the mind.

If your goal is to sharpen the mind and no purpose or meaning exists, you will fail along the journey of sharpening the short-term mind. Now ask, "What is your purpose? What is the meaning of your purpose?

What do you intend to do after you achieve your goal? What do you need to do to complete your mission? What are you to do after your mission is completed?"

Asking questions can open the mind to persuasion. In other words, asking questions can leave room in the mind to find answers. Still, you will need to deliberate after asking questions since it is the ultimate solution to finding answers.

One of the most disturbing things you see in people today is that people often find ways to ignore what goes on around them.

This is trapping the mind instead of working to sharpen the mind. We must face the fact that traumas, dramas, and bad memories will come our way in life. Facing the truth is the ultimate solution in unstrapping the mind and working to sharpen short-term memory. This is the process of coordinating and organizing the mind.

After you get past reality, you can work smoothly into keeping your mind sharpened. During the process, you want to learn to preview, review, recite, repeat, role play, visualizations, images, vision, sensory, mental capture, reconstruction, remove traps, and the like to sharpen the mind.

Externalized Thinking

Externalized thinking is an often overlooked strategy that can help with memory. It involves giving an external physical representation of an idea or concept, such as drawing a diagram or a map to represent something.

This allows your brain to make connections between information more visually and tangibly, leading to more effective recall when you need it.

Not only does this help cement the data into your memory, but it also helps maintain focus and a better understanding of the material. Furthermore, using externalized thinking exchanges memorization for spirited recollection and deep engagement with the material, creating an even stronger connection to the information you are trying to remember!

Externalized thinking is a powerful technique that can be used to improve your short-term memory. When trying to commit something important to memory, take the time to think through how best you could concretely output the information.

This could mean drawing a sketch or diagram showing the main points at a glance, making an imaginative mnemonic device, or even writing it down on paper.

Doing so can make it easier for your brain to store and retrieve the information since you'll be able to visualize what you're trying to remember or access other components of your intelligence, like creativity and lateral thinking.

It's also an incredibly effective strategy for studying, as externalized thinking helps make learning more engaging and tangible than simply repeatedly reading through pages of text. Invest some time into this approach and see your short-term memory skyrocket!

It's almost like having a whole other person there giving their opinion! First, try breaking the project into parts to employ externalized thinking.

Ask yourself questions like "What needs to be done in this situation?" and "What resources do I have access to?" Next, consider your options- do you have enough information to move forward, or do you need more? Finally, see if your inner circle can provide valuable insights and feedback.

Externalized thinking is beneficial for honing in on what's necessary - and it requires no additional effort! Even the best of us could use an extra viewpoint now and then.

Externally thinking your way to better memory takes some practice, but it can be a superb way to get the most out of your efforts and maximize the resources at hand.

Try writing down important items you need to remember by physically putting them on paper or imprinting them with a photo. This will help consolidate memories and enhance your recall.

Think about associating items you need to remember with something more meaningful, like a memorable phrase or an image, since our brains are naturally wired to remember visual pieces of information more. Finally, ask yourself questions about your learning to force yourself to recall the information and reinforce your comprehension.

Not only will this help you understand essential details better, but it will also dramatically improve your memory for long-term success.

Plenty of books available can help anyone learn how to put externalized thinking into practice and improve their memory.

With a quick search, you'll find resources like this materialize in no time and can unlock a world of knowledge about externalized thinking and memory improvement!

Concentration & Paraphrasing

Regarding our daily lives, having sharp short-term memory recall is invaluable. Not only does it help us to focus better on tasks and conversations, but it also enables us to remember important information more easily.

Next, we'll discuss the importance of sharpening your short-term memory recall skills, the benefits of "putting on those ears," and the concept of memory recall in general. Let's get started.

One of the best ways to sharpen your short-term memory recall skills is to focus on improving your listening skills. When communicating with someone else, please give them your full attention and try to understand what they are saying without interrupting them.

One tip is to paraphrase what they said back to them; studies have proved this to show that you understand what they are saying. It can also help verify facts discussed in conversations if you confirm them with a quick google search or two afterward.

Organizing Thoughts and Engaging Body Senses

Organizing thoughts and engaging body senses are two effective tools to use when trying to stay on task or have a productive conversation.

Taking a few deep breaths can help clear out any extraneous thoughts that may pop into your head while focusing, allowing you to concentrate better on the current task.

It's important to focus on the positives of your past experiences, even if they were less than ideal. Facing bad memories as a challenge rather than an obstacle allows you to move past negative experiences and keeps you motivated while pushing forward. Using simple breathing exercises or changing your thought process can be incredibly beneficial when refocusing your attention and maximizing productivity.

Clearing your mind while focusing on your breath can be done with a few simple steps. Firstly, find a comfortable and quiet place to sit or lie down without interruption.

Once ready, focus on each breath entering and leaving the body. If intrusive thoughts arise, acknowledge them but don't attach to them and instead focus back on your breathing. Make sure to be gentle with yourself if this practice is difficult at first; like any skill, mastering it takes practice and patience.

Continue this practice for up to five minutes or until you feel more in tune with your present-moment experience. This will help improve focus so you can make better decisions with clarity of thought.

One simple breathing exercise to help reduce stress and tension is the 4-7-8 breath technique. Firstly, sit or lie down in a comfortable position. Place one hand on your stomach and the other on your chest. Then, inhale deeply through your nose for four counts, ensuring that your stomach rises with each inhalation.

Hold this breath for seven counts before exhaling through your mouth for eight counts. Repeat this cycle as often as necessary until you feel more relaxed and present.

It is recommended to practice the breath focus for up to 5 minutes at a time, but you can adjust the duration depending on your available time. Start with shorter periods, such as 1-2 minutes, and gradually build up your duration until you feel comfortable holding your breath for longer periods.

Remember to be patient and gentle with yourself – mastering this skill will take practice and patience.

Here are some tips for being patient and gentle with yourself when practicing breathing exercises:

- Let go of any judgment or expectation of perfection – learning takes time, and you can't expect to be perfect immediately.
- Trust your timing; it's alright if you don't master the breath focus in the first few tries.
- Remind yourself that this practice will help you feel more relaxed, so stay positive and believe in your progress.
- Notice how your body feels when you'reholding your breath, then gently release as needed.
- Take breaks as needed - even if that means taking a break after just one minute of practice.

Recalling Information

When trying to improve your memory recall skills, one of the most important things is to separate relevant information from irrelevant information quickly and easily.

Try previewing tasks before jumping into action when ready; this allows you ample time to research facts about the topic to ensure all necessary information is included in whatever project or discussion you are embarking upon. Additionally, setting reminders for yourself regularly will help revive memories and ensure that nothing slips through the cracks!

From everyday life to the world of academia, the ability to remember fleeting pieces of information can be extremely useful. A study has found that simply donning a pair of "mouse ears"—such as those worn when visiting Disneyland or other amusement parks—can boost short-term memory performance.

The findings suggest that even small symbolic gestures, such as wearing costume accessories, can affect cognitive functioning. After all, wearing something as silly or unexpected as mouse ears might encourage us to think twice about what we're trying to commit to memory.

If you need quick recall, it's worth giving those comical ears a try!

Concentrating and listening cannot be overstated when storing information in the long-term. When these two activities are combined, they offer an unparalleled experience in retaining knowledge, skills, and memories for future use.

Focus on the task at hand is essential for fully comprehending what is being taught or presented; similarly important is the ability to pay attention and actively listen.

By doing so, not only does one benefit from gleaning every detail from the given material, but also by accurately recalling such information later on when needed.

Concentration and listening go hand-in-hand in making sure that any bits of data one wishes to remember are effectively cataloged for future reference in their mind.

Paraphrasing conversations are invaluable for honing one's language skills as it encourages thorough engagement with conversation.

Trying to repeat something said in different words or to re-emphasize something that has been said not only this aid in understanding words properly but also helps keep a conversation going and makes the speaker feel genuinely heard.

It may even encourage further growth in knowledge on a particular topic; by having the person who originated a statement explain more about their point of view, new insights—especially ones not noticed before—can be gained. All this from a strategy that only takes seconds to execute! In any language exchange situation, paraphrasing conversations is highly recommended for yielding maximum benefit.

In a world filled with misinformation, verifying facts is more important than ever when conversing with another person. Doing this helps us stay informed and is a great way to learn about different topics and stay up to date with current events.

Verifying facts through research or digging deeper into the source allows us to draw conclusions and form opinions. This is critical in our day and age as it helps us constantly expand our knowledge while avoiding misinformation that sways how we think. Simply put, verifying facts should be an integral part of the conversation so that minds can learn something new each time someone speaks.

Memory recall skills are an essential tool for most people; however, it often goes beyond habits of repetition or memorization. It is just as important to start a journey to short-term memory recollection by taking several preparatory steps.

First, organizing the thoughts and data allows for linear progression through tasks like research, summarizing the material, and organizing the order of information.

Engaging the body's senses, such as smell, touch, taste, and sight, allows us to further tangibly connect with whatever we are trying to recall. Avoiding battle with memories is also an important step in sharpening recalling skills, as ruminating over old painful events only distracts focus from the present.

Lastly, facing bad experiences may be intimidating but can offer a great opportunity to exercise memory recall skills and clarify the current situation or task at hand. Taking these steps before memorizing facts or data sets will set us up for successfully challenging our current knowledge base.

Recalling information is an important part of any task that requires a good understanding of the facts and data involved. It is essential to the process of being able to make wise decisions, complete tasks properly, and accurately recall information later.

Revoking and restoring information first helps people separate the facts from irrelevant data and ensures they have all the necessary information before they begin their task.

This memory rehearsal of facts also refreshes a person's knowledge of what was learned by refreshing their grasp on relevant material before jumping into action. This is why recalling information has become integral for anyone looking to be successful with their tasks or projects.

Total recall, memory, and remembering are all related but distinct concepts. Total recall is the power to remember incomplete details with complete clarity.

Memory is the power of the mind to process, store and retrieve information gathered later on. Remembering is a process of keeping the information in mind for later consideration. The human mind works like a computer in that it stores and retrieves data like our own hard drives.

The RAM or Random Access Memory resembles long-term memory since it serves as an internal storage area for data collected by the brain or computer. Short-term memory then bypasses storing information, holding onto it only momentarily before sending it off to the RAM for permanent storage - much like our long-term memory does.

The Read Only Memory (ROM) on computers holds programs that can't be changed, similar to short-term and long-term storage combined due to its relatively small size where only key details exist in memory.

Virtual memory also assists computers in storing data externally while associating internal storage with virtual storage within a machine's memory.

This parallels how humans use external associations to trigger meaning which helps sharpen their memories by adding additional data where needed - similarly, how caches work on computers as an encrypted environment for storing information, making them invaluable for developing better short-term memory skills over time.

Recalling people's names can be especially difficult even though we might have encountered them more than once, so understanding messages between those lines can help us move towards better understanding and sharpening our memories when recalling peoples' names along with other stored information we encounter during everyday life.

Remembering Names

Focusing on each person and paying full attention if you wish to remember their names is essential.

Try repeating the name in your head or even asking them to spell it back to you if need be. Visualization can be a powerful tool too - try picturing the name written somewhere on their clothing or body as they tell you what it is.

If you still struggle to remember, don't be afraid of asking them again and admit that you forgot their name - this will help ease any tension and give you a second chance at remembering.

Avoid letting yourself get caught up in negative trappers such as "I can't" or externalizing stressors - these only limit your potential for growth and learning.

By being conscious of these trappers and putting in some effort by repeating, visualizing, or asking politely for help with recall, you should see an improvement in your memory retention!

Visuals are an excellent way to remember names better. Firstly, try and come up with some physical characteristics or items associated with the person, such as clothes they may have worn, hairstyle, body parts like their nose or eyes - anything that has a unique feature that stands out to you.

You can also try associating objects or things related to the person's name - for example, if you just met Michael, you could recall his name by thinking of him wearing basketball shoes or pretending to shoot a basketball hoop.

Another fun association tactic is to use rhyming words or alliterations - if the person is named Amy, then think of her as "glamorous Amy" or something along those same lines. This will help your brain connect more easily between the name and its meaning.

Visualizing characters from books or films with similar names might also be helpful - maybe imagine Maggie from The Simpsons when you meet someone new called Maggie!

Remembering someone's name can be tricky, but here are a few tips to help you remember people's names better:

· Repeat and recite the name out loud - say hello to them and then repeat their name. Saying the name out loud helps embed it in your mind better.

· Ask them to spell or pronounce the name for you if needed; this will eliminate confusion about their spelling and help you better commit it to memory.

Try visualizing the person in your mind, write their name on their shirt, or use other associations that help you recall the name easily.

Use the person's name whenever possible during conversations - this will make it stick in your mind more easily over time.

If all else fails, politely ask them to repeat/spell/pronounce their name when you need a reminder - this could ease some of the tension if neither of you can remember!

It's common to forget someone's name, especially if you meet many new people. If this happens, try your best not to panic and be honest about the situation. If the person you are speaking to has a common name or is confused about their spelling or pronunciation, politely ask them for clarification. It may feel awkward, but it's better than pretending you know their name and getting it wrong!

You can also tactfully remind them of yourself by mentioning information that would jog their memory, such as where you met, any shared interests or experiences - anything that will help them recall who you are and how they know your name.

Finally, if all else fails, don't be afraid to politely laugh about it and admit that you have forgotten their name - despite the awkwardness of the situation, most people will usually understand and won't take offense!

One way to create an image association with a person in your mind is by making up a "story" or memory associated with them. For example, let's say you meet someone named Alex. You could imagine they are the star of a movie you saw where they were playing a scientist - so now you will remember them as the "scientist Alex."

You can also try associating the physical traits or characteristics of the person with something else. If they have long flowing hair, you could link that to Rapunzel in your mind, and now you will always remember them as "Rapunzel Alex."

This technique can also be used in other areas; for example, if you're trying to remember someone's profession, you could link it to an actor. If they are a doctor, imagine Hugh Laurie from House as the doctor instead!

Finding Creative Solutions

A person's mind can get trapped in anxiety and worry when faced with a difficult situation. Taking a step back and thinking logically about the problem is important before panicking.

Consider all available solutions, including calling for assistance if needed, and look for creative ways to solve the issue. This can help sharpen your memory as it forces you to actively engage your brain in finding possible solutions.

Facing difficult situations can be intimidating and make it difficult to think clearly. Here are a few tips to help sharpen your memory in these situations:

- Take a step back and try to assess the situation objectively. This will help you avoid getting overwhelmed and thinking of it as an impossible task.
- Make sure to take deep breaths and stay calm – this will allow you to remain focused on finding a solution without getting distracted by stress or anxiety.
- Break the problem into small, manageable tasks, so it is easier to focus on each individual.
- Actively engage your brain by actively looking for solutions – don't just sit back and wait for ideas to come to you, but go out and search for creative solutions.
- Consider all available options, even if they seem unlikely initially, as this can help spark new ideas that may not have occurred otherwise.
- Ask for assistance if needed; sometimes, talking with others can provide alternative perspectives and reveal insights that otherwise would not have been obvious.

Creative solutions to any issue can often provide insights and perspectives that may not have occurred to you before. Here are a few tips for brainstorming creative solutions:

- Try thinking outside the box and looking at the problem from different angles
- Set aside your assumptions about how things should be done and consider alternative approaches
- Take a step back and analyze what can be changed without altering the fundamental goal of the task
- Gather input from others by asking questions or seeking advice from experts in the field
- Challenge convention by considering unlikely options that could still lead to success

- Brainstorm in groups to generate new ideas through group collaboration

A logical approach to solving any problem involves understanding the scope of the issue and breaking it down into smaller, manageable parts. Here are a few tips for taking a logical approach:

- Gather all of the available information related to the problem
- Identify potential causes and take steps to identify which have the most impact
- Develop an action plan that outlines what needs to be done and in which order
- Prioritize tasks based on impact or importance
- Track progress and adjust your plan accordingly as needed
- Test different solutions systematically to ensure you select the most effective option

It's important to take regular breaks to step back and reassess your progress on any task. Set reminders for yourself so that you can pause, regroup, and gain a fresh perspective. If you find yourself repeatedly running into the same challenges, it may be time to rethink your approach or consider outside help.

When facing difficult situations, it can be helpful to sharpen your memory to recall the necessary information better. Here are a few tips for sharpening your memory:

- Keep a journal or other form of organized notes to refer back to
- Practice concentration and attention exercises such as yoga or meditation
- Test yourself with flashcards or memory games
- Take regular breaks and get enough sleep
- Make connections between related concepts and link them together in your mind
- Repeat key facts out loud or write them down for easier recall

Other Tips

It's important to sharpen your short-term memory in order to recall the necessary information when facing difficult situations. Here are a few tips you can use:

- Keep a journal or other form of organized notes to refer back to.
- Practice concentration and attention exercises such as yoga or meditation.
- Test yourself with flashcards or memory games.
- Take regular breaks and get enough sleep.
- Make connections between related concepts and link them together in your mind.
- Repeat key facts out loud or write them down for easier recall.
- Paraphrase when details need to be clarified in your mind.
- Review and preview before probing into new information.
- Learn to use visualization techniques to better understand what you've learned.
- Arrive at destinations earlier than scheduled if learning is involved.
- Concentrate on the talker and clarify the information delivered using paraphrasing, reciting, repeating, etc.
- Roleplay scenes to help you grasp deeper meaning and construct your mind building mindset.
- Learn about associations and how they will help you connect memories.
- Remove distractions or interruptions so that your mind can learn and remember effectively.

CHAPTER 4

The Four Parts of Memory

Memory is a powerful tool that allows us to store and recall important information. People look up to those with good memories because they can remember things better than others.

In this chapter, we'll look at how our memory works - how we can store and recall information. We'll learn how to create connections between ideas and facts to help us remember them better so that we can use what we know in our everyday lives.

Memory is an amazing thing! It helps us remember things that we have seen or learned. We can use memory to help us recall things from our past, like something we saw yesterday. We can also use it to remember things for the future, like important tests coming up. Memory is essential; without it, we wouldn't be able to do many of the things we need to do in our lives!

Memory comprises four main elements: retention, recall, imagination, and recognition. Retention is the ability to keep information in our minds and hold onto it for later use.

Recall is being able to remember the information when needed. Imagination helps us create mental images and associations with what we are learning to remember in the future. Lastly, recognition allows us to recognize patterns and familiar things that can help trigger our memory.

Together, these four elements help us store and retrieve information from our memories.

Different brain areas are essential for forming and holding on to memories. These areas include the hippocampus, prefrontal cortex, entorhinal cortex, striatum, and amygdala. The hippocampus is responsible for consolidating short-term memories into long-term experiences. The prefrontal cortex plays a role in storing long-term memories by creating associations between different pieces of information.

The entorhinal cortex helps us recall information from memory when needed. The striatum retrieves stored memories from our minds, and the amygdala helps create emotional connections to the memories we form. Together, these brain parts allow us to remember important things or facts.

Memory also involves communication taking place between the brain's vast networks of neurons and cells. Neurotransmitters are the chemicals that enable neurons to communicate and activate these millions of cells in the brain, which allows us to form memories. This complex process stores and retrieves information from our long-term memory.

Past Memories

Memory is thought of as our ability to recall and consciously reproduce ideas. Still, it also extends to the moments when thoughts or sensations from the past come unbidden into our minds.

This involuntary act of recollection is a form of memory as well. It is an essential and original power that not only serves as the source of all conscious life but binds it together too.

We know that impressions and sensations can remain etched in our memories even after they have been dormant for a long time. A particular scent, for example, can bring back all the emotions of a distant event with an intensity as strong as when it first occurred.

This is proof that, even after conscious sensation and perception have faded, their material remains can still be found in our nervous system, always ready to resurface in our minds.

Memory can be unreliable when retrieving certain things or events only experienced hurriedly once.

This is because when we recall these moments, the qualities shared by many things become detached from the objects they were connected to and gain an independent existence in our thoughts as ideas and conceptions. In this way, memory forms the basis of a large and diverse range of ideas and beliefs.

Memory is a complex process that involves not just consciousness but also unconsciousness. For example, vast periods of unconsciousness between our daily "selves" lie as we sleep or travel through the night. The connections between different impressions and memories in our brains are often quite orderly.

One thought can lead to another without each link being consciously regis-tered. As a result, the order in which ideas come to mind may differ from how they were experienced or processed initially. Nevertheless, it is still possible for us to recall long chains of memories without perceiving every step in the sequence.

Force of Habit

Memory is like a powerful glue that helps us to keep our thoughts, ideas, and experiences in one place. Without it, our minds would be scattered and disorganized.

Through the "force of habit," repeated actions become easier and easier to remember, allowing us to hold on to things longer and gather valuable knowledge from past experiences.

Memory may be intangible, but it plays an important role in keeping us focused, organized, and connected – all essential for living life to the fullest!

We all have the "force of habit" that helps us remember things easily. When we do something more than once, it becomes easier and easier to remember how to do it.

Memory, our mind's ability to remember, keeps us together in all the different things we experience daily. Without memory, we would be unable to keep our ideas and thoughts in one place or even move around the world.

Memory holds all our experiences together like glue; if it weren't for memory, our minds would be broken into tiny pieces!

It's like our memory is a muscle! If we use it more and more, it gets stronger. It's just like when you exercise - repeatedly doing the same thing means your muscles become stronger and better at doing that movement.

Your memory works analogously. When you use it, it becomes better and better at remembering things - plus, it also adds weight as it collects information for storage.

Our memory also grows and expands in size beyond its cells or fibers. It's not just a matter of them becoming stronger - it's also that more cells are being created.

This is especially true with plants, whose main job is to grow and develop, unlike animals with a wider range of capabilities. But the same principle applies - as we increasingly use our memory, it grows larger, encompassing added information and becoming better at recalling old facts.

Our brains and memory are much more delicate than physical muscles - we don't want to overload them. This is why it's important to put only a little strain on our mental capacity all at once, particularly when remembering things.

Instead of learning as much as possible in one go, we should gradually exercise our memory over time. That way, we can increase its capability without overtaxing our brains.

CHAPTER 5

What Everyone Believes

Most people believe that we only store memories in our mind, consisting of things we can remember upon will. In simple terms, they believe memory is confined to what we can recall.

However, this is an incorrect notion. Evidence from daily newspapers and magazines demonstrates cases where one's memory spontaneously lapses and recovers, serving as proof for the contrary.

Reasons for Forgetfulness

It is accepted that memory can be limited in its capacity. This limitation is due to our need for more power in voluntary recall. However, this does not imply that when we cannot call something to mind, it is always because the mental trace has been lost.

Often, memories remain dormant simply because we ignored them when they occurred in the first place - they were merely uninteresting or unimportant. The memories stay without enough associations or links to evoke them again.

Impact of Unperceived Sensations

Many of the sensations that come to us are ignored or unseen. This lack of attention causes us to overlook the influence of these subconscious impressions on our memory.

As a result, it is common for us to miss out on recalling experiences deemed unimportant when they initially occurred. This means that even though we believe we have forgotten certain events or occurrences due to our limited power of voluntary recall, they may remain just outside the confines of our conscious mind. These submerged memories can be activated by revisiting them with renewed effort and interest and uncovering the mental associations that once kept them hidden.

When we think of memory, we often focus solely on the importance of voluntary recall. However, it is equally important to consider the power of attention when preserving memories.

Just as different senses are attuned to a particular velocity or frequency when interpreting the world around us, people also tend to selectively focus on those elements that either have an immediate impact on them or relate more closely to their values and interests.

This means that whatever we pay special attention to has the potential to remain within our memories. At the same time, other experiences will be filtered out and forgotten over time.

All sensory impressions, somehow or other, leave their faint impression on the waxen tablets of the mind. Few are or can be voluntarily recalled.

Just where and how memories are retained is a mystery. Some theories represent sensory experiences as actual physiological "impressions" on the cells of brain cells. However, nothing but theories and how the brain, as the organ of the mind, keeps its record of sensory experiences has never been discovered.

Microscopic anatomy has never reached the point where it could identify a particular "idea" with anyone's "cell" or another part of the brain.

Memory and Attention

When we think about memory, it's easy to only think about how well we remember things. But it's also essential to consider the role of attention in preserving memories.

We all have five senses that help us experience the world around us – sight, hearing, touch, smell, and taste. These senses can be compared to a radio that picks up different frequencies or stories. Just like radio finds certain channels or stories, each person has a way of focusing on what's important to them.

What we focus on is likely to stay in our memories w, while other experiences might get filtered out. This means that even if something seemed unimportant initially, revisiting it with more effort or interest can uncover hidden memories that were stored away.

Have you ever had a moment when something suddenly feels familiar, even though you have never experienced it before? It's like your memory has been locked away. Still, suddenly, the right combination of events falls into place, and you remember something.

This is because we retain our sensory experiences, even if we weren't aware of them at the time. All the evidence shows that every sensation we've ever experienced is stored in our memory.

However, we may not always know how to access it. In other words, our minds are like treasure vaults with a wealth of facts. We must find the right way to open those doors and unlock all that knowledge!

CHAPTER 6

Recall Explained

Deep within every experience is a trigger - the key to unlocking the mysteries of memory retrieval. In exploring The Mechanism of Recall, we delve into the complex science that governs this process and how certain stimuli can activate memories and experiences long forgotten.

When you remember something, what's happening is that a bunch of things related to each other (ideas, feelings, muscular movements) is all connected.

These groups of related things are known as "complexes." For example, when you remember a happy experience from your childhood. It doesn't just mean that one memory pops into your head - it means lots of associated memories come into your head, too - like the sights and smells you experienced at the same time.

Right Stimulus

Sometimes, a single thought can bring us back to an old memory, and suddenly we feel a rush of emotions. For example, when you think about the time you were successful in a business deal, your body may react just like it did then - with a faster heartbeat, excitement coursing through your veins, and an overall feeling of triumph and joy. That is the power of recollection!

Imagine walking down the street and coming across a big, scary-looking building surrounded by fog with strange noises. You get a feeling of fear and start to sweat, and your heart starts to beat faster.

That feeling of fear is an example of what's known as a complex or functional derangement. It's a reaction that your mind must do something in your environment that it perceives as dangerous. It is like a reflex, where your body automatically responds to something that causes us to feel anxious or scared. Complexes and phobias can develop from traumatic events, such as experiencing earthquakes or being involved in robberies or murders.

When we remember these kinds of experiences, our bodies may again react the same way they did at the time — with trembling, perspiration, and palpitation of the heart — even if the incident is no longer happening. So when we experience things like this, we need to take care of ourselves and talk about our feelings if we need help processing them.

"Complexes" of Experience

In some cases, a complex phobia can lead to a functional disorder of the body. This is different from an illness that affects the physical body by damaging or destroying tissue – like a cut or broken bone.

A functional disorder is a problem with how efficiently our body functions in some way — like an inability to digest certain foods or difficulty sleeping properly. It might be caused by strong emotional or psychological responses, like those brought on by complexes and phobias, rather than by any physical injury or damage.

It's important to note that these issues can sometimes have serious long-term effects on your well-being. So if you notice any changes in your body's functioning, it's essential to talk about it with someone who can help.

The Thrill of Recollection

Humans have a wide range of experiences stored in their minds. They can have conscious thoughts and memories actively present in their minds and subconscious thoughts and memories that may not be consciously recalled but still affect behavior.

This is known as a complex or functional derangement. These include phobias, allergies, and physical reactions to specific triggers. For instance, two brothers might sneeze when they wake up in the morning even if they don't have a cold – conditioned responses to the morning routine could cause this.

Other functional derangements include hay fever, caused by outside factors such as dust or sunlight, and can cause inflamed nasal passages, coughing, and tears. It can even occur when someone looks at a paper rose instead of the real thing! All of this shows that our minds are amazing things, capable of forming connections between events and responses without us even being aware of them.

Recalling memories can be difficult, as many of them are stored in the subconscious.

Memories are experiences from the past that have been preserved by the human mind, like an impression on the wax cylinder of a phonograph. To recall these memories, it is necessary to use the process of recall – where past experiences are brought from the subconscious into consciousness.

This process is also done by associating unrelated ideas or objects. Recall can become more manageable with practice as our brains easily store and remember connections between events and stimuli.

Understanding how our brains form these connections can help us understand why specific topics or activities may unexpectedly bring back distant memories and experiences.

CHAPTER 7

Understanding the Laws of Recall

The first law of recall states that the recurrence or stimulation of one element in a complex can help to recall all others. This is important because it helps us remember things better and more effectively, allowing us to understand better what we are learning.

By actively recalling the components of a complex, we create meaningful connections between them that can be used for later recall. In other words, the more we practice recalling information from a complex, the easier it becomes to retrieve that information in the future.

The Law of Recall states that the recurrence or stimulation of one element in a complex can help to recall all other elements. This could mean actively recalling certain parts of a story, repeating a certain phrase to yourself multiple times, or even visualizing an image as you think about it.

This law helps us remember things better by creating meaningful connections between them, making it easier to access this information when needed. By actively engaging with and recalling a complex set of information, we can create strong ties that will serve as helpful reminders when trying to recall the information again.

The Law of Recall states that the recurrence or stimulation of one element in a complex can help to recall all other elements. This could mean actively recalling certain parts of a story, repeating a certain phrase to yourself multiple times, or even visualizing an image as you think about it.

This law helps us remember things better by creating meaningful connections between them, making it easier to access this information when needed. By actively engaging with and recalling a complex set of information, we can create strong ties that will serve as helpful reminders when trying to recall the information again.

One way to apply the first law of recall is to try and actively engage with the material you're trying to remember.

When studying for an exam, for example, actively recalling information from the text by summarizing it in your own words or creating mental images can help form meaningful connections between different pieces of information.

Additionally, repeating certain concepts or phrases multiple times can help commit them to memory. By engaging with information and revisiting it regularly, we can create stronger pathways of recollection that will allow us to access the information when needed.

Creating meaningful connections between different complex components can help later recall. One way to do this is to actively engage with the material, pick out key ideas and phrases, and create mental images and summaries that link the different components together.

Repeating certain concepts or phrases multiple times will further help commit them to memory. By repeating this process regularly and revisiting the material regularly, we create strong pathways that allow us to access the information later on when needed.

What Everyday Thinking is All About

Everyday mental processing typically consists of a collection of images connected and presented in succession.

Suppose, for instance, you witness a flower tucked inside the pages of a textbook – this could cause recollections to surface regarding the individual who gifted it to you. Thus transporting your mind back to when last you were with them and furthering reflections about their hometown.

This sequence of thoughts could lead to considering the railroad construction in progress and drawing daydreams about a future excursion to the beach.

Inevitably, many everyday contemplations are composed of this similar chain reaction centered around customary links or relations. Yet if your correlations are uncommon or unusual, one is said to have a mind full of wit and creativity.

The Law of Association

The Law of Association is integral to understanding human behavior and experience.

It explains how ideas become linked, allowing us to recall related information quickly. This can be incredibly helpful when faced with difficult tasks or situations - enabling us to draw upon our past experiences for new insights and solutions.

However, it is important to find the right balance between providing too much information, which leads to lengthy conversations or explanations, and not enough, which confuses.

By combining terseness with the ability to bring up meaningful details, we can effectively communicate our thoughts without wasting too much time.

Leveraging the Law of Association efficiently involves using it to draw upon previous experiences for new insights and solutions.

For example, when facing a particular issue at work, one can use this law to recall related information quickly, such as customer feedback or previous solutions that were implemented successfully.

This can help save time and effort when searching for answers. Additionally, it's important to find the right balance between providing too much information (which leads to long conversations) and not enough (confusing).

By combining terseness with an ability to bring up meaningful details, we can effectively communicate our thoughts without wasting too much time.

Finding the right balance between providing too much information and not enough when communicating thoughts is key. It's important to provide enough information to get the point across without getting lost in unnecessary details.

This can be done by using concise language, focusing on the most relevant details, and avoiding jargon or overly complex words that might confuse others. Additionally, by clearly explaining why certain points are important and how they relate to the conversation, one can ensure that their thoughts are fully understood. Lastly, checking in regularly with those involved in the conversation helps ensure everyone is on the same page and understands what is being discussed.

The Law of Contiguity

People remember things differently based on their experiences. The more often an experience is encountered and the stronger the feelings associated with it, the more likely it will be remembered. This is known as the Associative Law of Contiguity.

The Associative Law of Contiguity states that people will make connections between items or events that are either similar or close in proximity. This means that the more frequently an experience is encountered and the stronger the associated feelings, the easier it is to recall.

By connecting different elements of our experiences, we can better remember them.

Associative memory is remembering experiences and relationships between different elements of our experiences. According to the Associative Law of Contiguity, when two items or events are similar or close together, people will more easily connect them.

This can help us recall memories associated with these experiences much faster than if we didn't have this type of relationship between them. For example, if you're learning a foreign language, it may be easier to remember certain words if they are associated with objects or images you already know.

Experiences can have a major impact on our memory. Strong emotional connections to certain experiences make it easier to recall them.

For example, if you had a traumatic childhood experience, you will likely remember it more vividly than other events or memories from your life. Similarly, positive emotions associated with experiences can help us remember them in greater detail and more accurately.

Additionally, repeating something multiple times can help to memorize it because we become acclimated to the information and can recall it more readily during future encounters.

One way to remember things better is by using associations. Associations involve creating a connection between two items or concepts.

Connecting ideas, objects, or people with a visual image, sound, action, or location can do this. For example, if you are studying for an exam and want to remember certain concepts, you could associate them with images that remind you of that concept.

Additionally, repeating the concepts multiple times can help them stick in your memory better than just reading them once.

Associations can be used in everyday life in a variety of ways. For example, to remember where you parked your car, you might associate the car with a mental image of the location, such as the street intersection or store you were near.

You could also use associations to remember items on your grocery list by associating each item with an image or something that reminds you of it.

Another way to use associations is to remember people's names; when you meet someone, connect the person's name with an image or sound that will help you recall it later.

Associative Laws of Habit and Intensity

The Associative Laws of Habit and Intensity explain how certain habits and memories can be easily stored and recalled.

To summarize, these laws state that habits are strengthened with repetition, the intensity of a habit increases with the strength of emotion attached to it when two items are associated, each will recall the other more quickly, and finally that associations made for a longer period are more likely to be remembered.

Repetition is an important factor when forming habits, as it helps to strengthen and reinforce the habit. Repeating an action or thought over time reinforces connections in our brains and strengthens the neural pathways associated with that habit.

This makes it easier for us to recall the habit in future situations, as it has become more ingrained in our memory. Additionally, repetition can help to create strong positive associations with the habit, making it even more likely for us to recall it when needed.

One example of two items that can be associated is color and emotion.

Different colors often evoke certain emotions in people, such as blue being associated with calmness and yellow being associated with happiness. People may experience these emotions more strongly when exposed to the color or when they think about it.

For example, looking at a bright yellow flower might induce joy and contentment.

Here are some research-backed tips on how to make a habit easier to stick to:

- Start small - break big tasks into smaller, more achievable steps and focus on forming one habit at a time.
- Create accountability - involve others in your goal by sharing it with them or enlisting their help and support in achieving it.
- Tell yourself "why" - remind yourself of the importance of the end goal when things get tough, why you're working towards this particular habit, and what benefits it will bring.
- Make it enjoyable - find ways to make the task more fun or enjoyable, such as setting rewards for each success achieved or changing the environment in which you complete the task.
- Track progress and reward yourself - use a tracking system such as a calendar or chart to visibly track progress, and give yourself rewards each time you reach a benchmark or milestone.

Advertising & Recall

The Laws of Recall are especially relevant when it comes to advertising. Even the best-written and well-illustrated promotion.

It may only be worth its cost if one understands the fundamental principles behind choosing a location, picking a medium, and calculating how large an ad should be. Advertisers in metropolitan newspapers and magazines of wide circulation have the most to gain.

No matter what audience you are trying to reach. It would be best to keep specific facts rooted in psychological experiments about laws of recall at the forefront of your mind.

Though advertisers often understand that certain spots on a page are more desired than others, they need to grasp the actual distinction in recall value. Space in significant publications is a costly expense, yet the worth of such knowledge is undeniably valuable. Numerous tests have determined that recall value increases significantly depending on where it appears on an individual page.

For instance, studies show that placing content in the upper-right corner has more than double the impact compared to its location in the bottom left-hand corner.

The Effect of Repetition

While many advertisers prefer to blitz full-page ads with long breaks in between, laboratory tests have revealed that a quarter-page advertisement appearing consecutively for four weeks is 50% more effective than one single full-page ad.

Thus, spacing out your promotions can be the key to visibility and success.

Contrary to popular belief, running an eighth-page advertisement eight times is not necessarily more successful; its effectiveness may diminish if the ad appears too small. Some specific promotions or events warrant a full-page or double-page spread for maximum impact.

Nonetheless, these situations comprise only a fraction of all advertising campaigns - ultimately making smaller ads more cost-effective and reliable for businesses to gain exposure.

The Ratio of Size to Value

Inadvertently, billions of dollars are wasted in the United States yearly on advertising commodities without any scientific consideration. Not only is there a risk of a total loss, but also potential damage due to inadequately constructed and mispositioned advertisements.

As advertisers, we must recognize the impactful research psychologists have conducted and continue to conduct regarding this topic so that our money is spent effectively.

- Companies usually opt for full-page ads at wide intervals. Still, research has uncovered that a quarter-page ad appearing in four consecutive paper issues is fifty percent more successful.
- Nonetheless, it's important to note that the value of an advertisement diminishes much faster than the cost when its dimension drops below a certain level.
- Every year in the United States, billions of dollars are recklessly poured into advertising various goods without any real scientific understanding or insight on how to effectively build and display them for maximum success.
- Psychologists are striving to gain exact comprehension and facts about this field to help advertisers make informed choices when investing in marketing endeavors.

CHAPTER 8

Focus

The power of attention is often overlooked, but it is an invaluable tool for improving our mental faculties. Particularly our capacity to remember things, focus on essential tasks, and form habits that come naturally to us over time.

What is Attention?

Attention refers to the process by which we can recall experiences and memories from our past. It also constructs awareness by selecting related groups of experience which become part of our conscious memory storehouse.

This process allows us to selectively focus on certain facts relevant to our aims while disregarding others to draw more meaningful conclusions about a given situation or event that has occurred in our lives or those around us.

The power of attention also enables us to improve our capacity to remember information quickly and accurately. This is through familiarizing ourselves with topics or ideas we may have encountered or are likely to encounter again.

How Does Attention Work?

Attention works according to the Laws of Recall, allowing us to retrieve memories from long-term storage or short-term working memory easily and efficiently when needed for decision-making processes or problem-solving activities required throughout our day-to-day lives.

It also plays a crucial role in forming habits. It deliberates that concentration and attention must be practiced until they eventually become unconscious activities occupying a semi-automatic middle ground between conscious and subconscious activities. Hence, it enables us to carry out tasks without overthinking them beforehand.

This happens when they eventually become second nature with the consistent effort put into practice these new skillsets acquired—made possible through obtaining knowledge within different domains of expertise you wish to expand upon further down the line!

Benefits of Attention

Numerous advantages are associated with exercising one's ability for attentive behavior beyond simply recalling memories better. Improved powers of focus & concentration can lead directly to formulating better plans.

This also includes taking proper action steps towards accomplishing goals from newly obtained growth mindset shifts along with higher productivity due. Based on honing your skillset within even more specific niches, efficiency measures are also taken into account.

Ultimately comprising an impressive repertoire everyone should strive towards develop further within their respective journeys ahead! Furthermore, regular practice makes perfect when implementing new tactics garnered from learning something new.

Repetition helps develop one's unawareness slowly yet surely until desired outcomes manifest themselves, most likely sooner than later in the grand scheme of things, alongside other factors taken into consideration before actually starting!

Strategies for Practicing Attention

There are numerous techniques available for practicing one's ability for attentive behavior. Meditation techniques such as mindfulness meditation can help increase focus while decreasing distractions created externally.

Completing regular tasks that require attention & focus, such as reading, can help improve mental acuity & stimulate cognitive functions associated with memory recall.

Setting goals & successfully achieving them can provide a sense of accomplishment, which fosters self-discipline & facilitates enhanced self-control over impulses. This could distract us from reaching objectives set beforehand, whether short-term or long-term, depending on each individual's circumstances assessed thoroughly, also included during this process itself! All these practices come together hand-in-hand.

Providing tangible results anyone striving towards excellence endures during their journey down understanding, gaining more significant insights along the entire ride through sheer persistence pay off handsomely, indeed invariably speaking.

The power of attention cannot be understated when it comes to living a productive, fulfilling life with whole meaning and purpose beyond merely existing.

Increased memory recall capabilities allow better decision-making processes to lead to successful outcomes desired. At the same time, becoming aware and focusing on essential tasks shows increased levels of productivity overall.

Perhaps the only benefit gained here alone suffice to say to do so accordingly afterward! To summarize all said and done prior mentioned, general gist practice regularly remaining mindful, staying present moment, enjoying every second counts times almost here never forgetting to appreciate everything received behold shortly after that after all.

CHAPTER 9

Don't Memorize

It is often assumed that memorization and practice is the only way to improve memory, but that is not true. Focusing on the proper use and understanding of information is more important than the practice of memorizing it.

Retaining the information for longer periods will be easier when you develop an intense interest in the content you're studying. However, diffused attention or a lack of interest can lead to forgetfulness and unprofitable results. So, what are some strategies for improving your memory?

The first step is to identify and focus on your goals and intentions. Understanding why you need this information will help narrow your focus and allow you to retain more information.

Visualization techniques can also be beneficial when trying to remember something; picturing yourself retrieving facts from your mind can help embed them into your long-term memory.

It helps to relate new information to existing knowledge or experiences to build a stronger mental connection with it.

Active recall strategies are also helpful when remembering something;

repetition, summarization, elaboration, and other mnemonic devices can help recall if done correctly. Exercise has also been proven to increase brain function and boost concentration levels.

At the same time, quality sleep refreshes memory centers so that new information can be retained better. Finally, developing a learning routine or schedule helps establish a systematic approach to acquiring knowledge so that it becomes easier over time.

The Science

There is a science behind memory retention; understanding how your brain processes and stores data is critical to developing effective memorization methods that work for you.

With the right combination of effort and technique, anyone can improve their memory skills regardless of age or experience!

Developing an intense interest in the content being studied, combined with active recall strategies such as repetition or visualization, will make learning faster and easier over time, so you don't have to rely solely on memorization anymore!

You should identify and focus on your goals and intentions to improve your memory. This will help you narrow your focus, enabling you to retain the information better. Additionally, understanding why you need certain information can motivate you to remember it better and for longer periods.

Understanding why you need a particular piece of information can help motivate you to learn and remember it better, as well as for longer periods. Knowing the value or importance of the information can give you a goal to focus on, enabling you to retain the data more efficiently.

Additionally, understanding why this information is valuable can help you relate it to existing knowledge or experiences, which can further increase retention rates.

Strategies

Relating new information to existing knowledge or experiences can help you remember it better.

Drawing connections between the two can form a more concrete understanding of the data and how to use it in different situations. It can also help you contextualize the new piece of information, which can make recall easier in the future.

Connecting a relevant experience can motivate you to remember the data more meaningfully.

Once you've committed information to memory, it's important to recall it actively. Through active recall strategies, such as repetition, summarization, elaboration, and mnemonic devices, you can more effectively retain the information and ensure it's recalled accurately in the future.

Regular physical exercise has increased brain function and concentration, aiding in memorization and recall.

Repetition is a primary active recall strategy for memorization, as it helps to reinforce the data that has been learned. By repeating the information out loud or writing it down several times, you can store and solidify it in your memory.

Spaced repetition—or rehearsing information at increasingly wider intervals—is one of the most effective strategies for retaining knowledge.

Summarization is another active recall strategy that can help to improve memorization. With summarization, you break down large amounts of information into smaller, more easily digestible chunks and review them as a summary.

By restructuring the data into simpler, more organized concepts, it can be easier to remember what was covered and recall the information later.

Elaboration is a strategy that can help to improve memory recall. It involves using associations and connections to help strengthen the link between the material being learned and the person's existing knowledge.

For example, suppose someone was trying to remember a particular date. In that case, they may associate that date with something else, such as an event or personal landmark. Making these connections and expanding on them can make recalling the information from memory easier when needed.

Mnemonic devices are tools that can be used to increase memory retention. This can involve using rhymes, catchphrases, visual images, mental associations, and more to help recall information quickly and easily.

Creating these connections and creatively using them makes it easier to remember large amounts of data for longer periods.

Developing a regular learning routine or schedule can help you stay focused and engaged when studying. Start by setting aside a specific amount of time you dedicate to learning each day. It can be helpful to plan out what topics you will cover during this time and break them down into small, achievable goals.

It is important to use an effective combination of effort and technique when studying to maximize efficiency and results. Break down complex topics into smaller, more manageable chunks to get started.

Take notes while reading or listening to lectures, and form questions you can use to test your understanding of the material. Practice active recall by periodically summarizing what you have learned to reinforce the information.

Utilize time management strategies such as setting deadlines and breaking large tasks into smaller tasks with actionable steps. Finally, challenge yourself by seeking additional sources of information on the subject matter to deepen your understanding.

When studying, there is no need to rely solely on memorization. Instead, focus on understanding the material fully by analyzing and interpreting what you are learning.

Ask yourself questions about the content and think critically about how it relates to other topics or concepts.

Try to view complex topics from different perspectives, as this can help provide a comprehensive understanding of the subject matter. Finally, include diverse sources such as videos, podcasts, and articles in your studies - these can be more engaging than text-based resources.

CHAPTER 10

Business Success

The ability to recall facts, figures, and data are critical to business success. We are bombarded with information, and it cannot be easy to store it all in our minds. Let's take a closer look at how this system works.

Increasing Memory Associations

This is done using Figure-Alphabet, which allows us to link numbers with words or pictures, making them easier to remember. For example, if you wanted to remember the number "23," you could associate it with "two cats" or "a banana split," both of which would help make remembering the number 23 much easier.

Efficient Pedagogy also helps create memory associations by linking facts together through association in an efficient manner. This allows us to recall information more efficiently as we have developed stronger pathways between related facts.

Thought-Memory Training Exercises

To further develop observation and thought-memory training exercises, five exercises have been created to develop observation skills, such as comparing two objects side by side or observing an object while blindfolded.

Three exercises have been created for thought-memory training, such as memorizing a list of items in order or taking notes from a lecture without looking at them until after the lecture has finished.

Examples of these exercises include memory games where you try to memorize as many words as possible from a list or create a story based on several objects presented in front of you and then try to recite the story back word for word after several minutes have passed.

Building Correct Memory Habits

The rules that must be followed for one's memory habits leading towards business success to become correct habits that will prove successful long term, such as making systematic use of sense organs (i.e., sight, sound, smell, etc.), fixing ideas by their associates (creating strong links between related concepts), searching systematically and persistently (not giving up when faced with difficulty), and taking immediate action upon recollection being made (acting on newfound knowledge).

Creating and Maintaining Good Memory Habits

When a task comes to mind, act immediately. Every thought that pops into your head is meant to be acted upon; if you don't take advantage of the moment, it could slip away forever. Take your time tomorrow when it may already be too late – seize the day! If you heed your mental prompts and act on them, they will help guide you reliably.

ACT NOW

This is as true of bodily habits as of business affairs. The time to act upon an important matter that just now comes to mind is not "tomorrow" or a "little later," but NOW. Being aware of the decisions you make in your daily life can have a massive impact on your career trajectory.

When new ideas come to you, you must evaluate which ones are most meaningful and applicable to your current goals. Be honest when judging new opportunities and determine what is worth pursuing.

Do not be swayed by distracting impulses that inadvertently slip in. And having gauged their importance gives free rein at once to the impulse to do everything that should not make way for something more important.

Perseverance, Precision, and Promptness

If, for whatever reason, you need to postpone acting on something, be sure to commit it firmly to memory. Put all other thoughts aside and concentrate solely on this matter. Decide when you want to remember it and put your full energy into ensuring that you will recall it at exactly the right time.

Make sure you have some tangible reminders. This sign or token can be whatever you choose if it is inextricably linked to the hour that the main event must be remembered.

Memory-Making Mementos!

Preserve the precious memories that matter to you by creating personalized tokens and signs.

Establish a pattern of maintaining these symbols as reminders for yourself, then label the things most important to your recollection with tags or markers.

Allow them to become an integral part of how you process information in your mind!

Cultivate the practice of undertaking tasks when they ought to be finished and in their appropriate sequence – these habits create "paths" that your mind can follow easily, leading you towards success. These paths promote punctuality, vigor, determination, precision, self-discipline, and more.

To be successful in business and life, one must form strong habits. Creating a habit takes intentional work, persistently doing something until it becomes natural and second nature. Only when you've done this can you truly benefit from the rewards of developing positive routines.

CHAPTER 11

Brain Power & Brain Health 101

Brain health and power are often interchangeable, but they're not the same. This chapter will explain their key differences and what you're trying to improve when exploring this subject matter.

Brain health equates to a well-functioning, healthy brain capable of easily managing daily tasks. Brain power relates to the capacity for learning, memory recall, processing information quickly, and having good decision-making skills.

Both brain health and brain power are essential for optimal functioning; therefore, it's important to create a balanced regimen that focuses on nourishing both areas.

Maintain Healthy Cognition

The key to brain health is to function optimally during daily activities, such as work. This encompasses making sound decisions, solving problems effectively, maintaining emotional stability, and interacting successfully with others.

All these skills rely on remembering things, comprehending new information, learning quickly, processing data efficiently, thinking creatively, and being innovative when problem-solving. Note that brain health is not merely the function itself. Rather, brain health refers to the state of your brain that allows it to carry out those functions properly.

Unfortunately, unhealthy lifestyles combined with accidents can lead to a brain that does not function optimally. Our brains constantly change and adapt when we think, learn, imagine, and feel. These changes can be impacted by the habits you choose to keep throughout your life. We all need to take an active role in preserving good brain health!

The World Health Organization's Insights

Good brain health is essential to maximize the functioning of your emotional, psychological, behavioral, and cognitive abilities throughout your life.

Several interconnected biological and social determinants influence brain health and development, including pre-conception through end-of-life factors. These can determine how our brains develop, respond to situations, and adapt to changes.

To ensure good brain health, you should focus on creating a balanced lifestyle that includes a nutritious diet, regular exercise, plenty of sleep, stress management techniques such as yoga or meditation, staying socially active, avoiding unhealthy habits like smoking or drinking alcohol excessively, and engaging in activities that stimulate memory recall and cognitive functioning.

Brain health conditions can occur across the life course, manifesting as neurological and neurodevelopmental conditions—such as headache, multiple sclerosis, Parkinson's disease, neuroinfectious, autism spectrum disorders, cerebrovascular disease, brain tumors, epilepsy, cerebral palsy, dementia, traumatic injury and neurological disorders caused by malnutrition.

To prevent issues from arising and make progress across the life course, it is important to focus on adopting healthy lifestyle strategies that include a nutritious diet, regular exercise, adequate sleep (7-9 hours a night), managing stress through yoga or meditation methods, staying socially active and avoiding unhealthy habits such as smoking or drinking alcohol excessively.

Engaging in activities that stimulate memory recall and cognitive functioning can help maintain good brain health.

It is important to adopt a multisectoral, interdisciplinary approach focusing on prevention, well-being promotion, treatment, and care for individuals to provide social and health care for brain health conditions.

Rehabilitation should also be considered over the lifespan and involve people experiencing the condition along with their families and carers when necessary. A holistic person-centered approach will ensure the best possible outcomes while providing personalized care to those affected by these conditions.

Indeed, brain health and brain power are not the same things. Brainpower is all about intelligence and the ability to think - what we admire most in people. It requires having a high level of cognitive function, allowing you to stay ahead in a world where physical strength and muscle power are becoming less important.

Low brain power isn't an option if you want to succeed in today's highly competitive world, so make sure you look after your brain health and invest in activities that help stimulate memory recall and cognitive functioning.

To be successful in the modern world, you don't need to have the most physically demanding job. Instead, it's about having a sharp mind and maximizing your brain power to perform at your highest level.

With countless people looking to replace you for failing to produce the goods, you must remain focused, alert, and deliberate in improving your cognitive ability. Ideas such as playing memory games, learning new skills, reading complex books, and taking classes are great ways to strengthen your mental capacity over time.

Did you know that the human brain is a fascinating, complex organ? Some truly incredible facts about it may surprise you. Here are just a few!

High brain power isn't just essential to competing in the modern world; it can guarantee that you can get more done quickly. Some people are naturally super intelligent.

While this cannot be replicated, everyone can increase their cognitive ability and stay one step ahead. The Brain Health Index (BHI) is an excellent way to objectively measure your brain's performance - it allows you to scientifically track changes in your mental capacity and subjectively detect when your brain performance is improving.

Making sure you engage in activities like memory games, learning new skills, reading complex books, and regularly taking classes can help strengthen your mental power and keep your brain functioning at its best.

As this section winds down, let us take a moment to explore some fun facts about the brain. From its impressive abilities to its unique anatomy, here are some interesting tidbits you may find intriguing before we discuss maintaining cognitive health and boosting mental prowess.

Remarkable Lengths of Blood Vessels

Astoundingly, the brain contains more than one hundred thousand miles of blood vessels - that's nearly four times longer than the entire circumference of Earth!

If you stretch out all those vessels as a journey worldwide, it will take days to complete. Such an immense network is necessary for allowing us to think and function in our everyday lives.

Roaming Thoughts Are Natural

Maintaining focus is essential for success. However, it is perfectly normal to find yourself lost in thought occasionally. Research has demonstrated that certain brain parts are responsible for governing activities such as daydreaming - and these regions remain active even when your mind is at rest!

Thinking is an oxygen-heavy task. When engaging in serious thought, up to 50% of the brain's oxygen reserves can be used - making it especially important to reduce anxiety and keep your brain functioning properly.

Engaging in activities like walking, taking a bath, or participating in yoga can help reduce stress levels and ensure that your brain gets the oxygen it needs to stay healthy.

It's also important to give yourself regular breaks throughout the day so that your mind has time to rest and recuperate, allowing you to perform at your best when engaging in mental activities.

The size of your brain doesn't necessarily equate to intelligence. Despite popular belief, no scientific evidence suggests that a larger brain will make an individual smarter or more capable.

The shape and complexity of the brain are far more important than its size when it comes to cognitive ability. Activities like reading complex books, memorizing facts and data, and challenging yourself with puzzles can help keep your brain functioning at its peak, regardless of size.

Have you ever wondered what the human brain would feel like if you touched it? The middle adult human brain weighs around 3 pounds and has a texture that can be compared to firm jelly. It's an interesting thought to consider and one which makes understanding and appreciating the complexity of the brain even more fascinating!

The brain is quite a powerhouse and carries out an incredible number of activities within a short period. It's not surprising then that it consumes a high amount of blood, with up to 25% of all blood pumped by the heart going straight to the brain! Considering how much energy and oxygen are required for such complex thinking processes, it makes sense.

Our brains are very complex, consisting of an intricate web of connections. Every action carried out by other body parts is a product of these connections in the brain.

Take, for example, our ability to recall thoughts - this would not be possible without the connections and pathways created between neurons in the brain! Amazingly, such a vast array of ultra-connected networks allow us to do basic functions like walking and more complicated problem-solving.

Our brains are made up of over 100 billion neurons, accounting for 10% of our brain mass. To put this into context, a single neuron can connect to 10,000 others!

These connections form a vast array of neural pathways, which experts call the neuron forest. This immense complexity allows us to do anything from simple motor functions like walking to more complicated activities like problem-solving.

CHAPTER 12

Enhancing Cognitive Function

Scientists have conclusively proven that it can boost brain health and power. Food and exercise are key components to enhancing brain power and health. In this chapter, we'll dig deeper into the science behind how these two factors help our brains stay healthy and maximize their potential.

From boosting specific neurotransmitters to developing new neural pathways, the evidence is clear that food and exercise can make a real difference in how we think, act, and feel.

Feeding Your Brain

It is no wonder why the saying "we are what we eat" holds so much truth.

Nutrition plays a vital role in many aspects of our lives, from emotions to brain health. Our brains are constantly working, even when we're sleeping, which is why it needs an energy supply that they can draw on throughout the day.

The food we eat provides this fuel and can significantly impact how our brains function and the structure they take on. In turn, this affects many parts of our bodies, both cognitively and emotionally.

As Harvard Medical School so aptly put it, your brain is like an expensive car that needs premium fuel to perform at its highest. It is essential, then, that we give our brain all the nutrition it needs in the form of minerals, vitamins, and antioxidants.

These nutrients nourish and protect the brain from oxidative stress - a condition caused by free radicals produced when oxygen is used, which can damage body cells. And just like an expensive car, if you don't properly take care of your brain with high-quality foods and top-notch fuel, it can suffer long-term consequences.

You need to take the necessary steps to provide your brain with the most nutritious fuel to avoid experiencing cognitive impairment and memory loss.

You may also need help with motor coordination and problem-solving. Furthermore, mood swings, depression, and higher stress levels can all be attributed to poor nutrition.

Ultimately, not caring for your brain properly can lead to health issues that could have easily been avoided by eating high-quality foods and giving them the premium fuel it needs.

Not only is it important to give your high-quality brain fuel, but it's also essential to avoid substances that could damage it. For example, diets high in refined sugars are harmful to the brain.

They can worsen your body's regulation of insulin, which promotes oxidative stress and inflammation - both of which can lead to impaired brain function.

Furthermore, these foods can exacerbate the symptoms of mood disorders such as depression. So if you want to keep your mind healthy and sharp, it's best to steer clear of refined sugars and processed foods.

It's important to provide high-quality nutrition to keep your brain healthy and sharp. Diets high in refined sugars and processed foods can lead to a buildup of free radicals, damaging brain tissue and impairing brain function.

Deprivation of essential nutrients can contribute to brain tissue injury and impair brain power. Therefore, focusing on nutrient-rich foods that support optimal brain health is best.

Your Emotional Intelligence

Did you know that the foods you eat can impact your emotional intelligence? This is because a neurotransmitter in your brain called serotonin helps regulate sleep, appetite, moods, and pain inhibition. Around 95% of this neurotransmitter is produced in the gastrointestinal tract - an area lined with around 100 million nerve cells, meaning that it not only digests food but also plays a role in how we feel emotionally. Consequently, what you eat can greatly impact how you respond to situations and how emotionally balanced you are.

Did you know that the beneficial bacterium in your gut plays a role in influencing the functions of serotonin and, subsequently, emotional intelligence?

These bacteria protect the lining of your intestines, limit inflammation, improve nutrient absorption from food, and activate neural pathways between your brain and the gut. These bacteria are essential for maintaining good health, with impacts beyond digestion.

Research has indicated that people who stick to traditional diets, such as the Mediterranean diet, have a decreased likelihood of suffering from depression compared to those who eat a typical Western diet - which is 25-30% more likely to result in mood disorders.

This is because traditional diets are rich in vegetables, unprocessed grains, fruits, seafood, and lean meats while steering clear of refined foods and sugars. The presence – or lack thereof – of these foods may play a role in how prone you are to developing depression and other mood disorders.

Switching up your diet could be a great way to experience firsthand the impact of food on emotional intelligence.

For one month, try eating only Western foods and document your feelings in a journal – then switch to traditional foods for the next month and compare how you feel! You may find that when you eat higher quality, nutritious foods, not only do you benefit from improved brain health, but you also find your emotional intelligence soaring.

Exercise & Well-being

Working out isn't just a great way to stay in shape – regular physical activity has also been proven to boost cognitive abilities. Neuropsychologist Aaron Bonner-Jackson explains that exercise affects the body and does wonders for the brain.

The next time you hit the gym or run, remember that it's making your body healthier and improving your brain health!

An impressive study involving 454 older adults showcased the effects of regular physical activity on cognition. After wearing accelerometers to track their movements around the clock, it was found that those who moved more scored higher in memory and thinking tests over twenty years.

Those who were more physically active were at 31% lower risk of suffering from dementia even when factoring in brain pathology – proving the lasting impact of exercise on a person's mental well-being!

A recent study of 160 sedentary older people suffering from mild cognitive impairment found even more proof of exercise's role in improving mental well-being.

Only those who combined the Dietary Approaches to Stop Hypertension (DASH) diet with exercise showed notable improvements in their problem-solving and decision-making abilities. Exercise is an invaluable part of maintaining good mental health!

There's no one silver bullet in enhancing brain power and mental health - it's often a combination of different lifestyle factors.

Our brains are like computers; just like computers, they need proper care and maintenance to stay healthy. Eating certain foods can help boost your brain power and help you think better. These foods contain nutrients that keep your brain functioning as it should. For example, omega-3 fatty acids are found in some fish and nuts.

They help keep your brain cells healthy, promote clear thinking, and improve memory. Foods high in iron and zinc, such as beef, beans, spinach, eggs, and fortified cereal, can also help mental performance. Exercising is also important for overall health, especially keeping your brain in shape.

Regular exercise increases blood flow to the brain, which helps with concentration and focus and reduces stress levels. Lastly, reducing stress is important in maintaining good mental health because our brains do not work properly when we're stressed. So, take time each day to relax and enjoy yourself – it's good for both body and mind!

If your mind and body don't take the right care, you could risk experiencing highs and lows. Eating the right foods can help to fuel your brain, giving it the energy it needs to think clearly. Fish, nuts, beef, beans, spinach, eggs, and fortified cereal provide essential nutrients to maintain good mental health. Exercise is also important for keeping your brain sharp and reducing stress levels. Plus, taking breaks throughout the day can help relax you so that your whole body and mind can stay as healthy as possible!

Eating foods with Omega-3 fatty acids is a great way to help boost your brain power and promote clear thinking. Foods rich in omega-3s, such as fish, nuts, eggs, and fortified cereals, help keep your brain cells healthy and improve memory.

Regular exercising can increase blood flow to the brain, which enables you to think clearly and focus better while reducing stress levels. Combining a balanced diet with regular physical activity can go a long way in helping people stay physically and mentally healthy!

Eating regular meals and getting enough sleep are essential for maintaining good mental and physical health. Eating a balanced diet with lots of fruits, vegetables, fish, nuts, eggs, and fortified cereals can provide your body and brain with the nutrients it needs to function properly.

Also, supplementing your diet with vitamins such as zinc or folic acid helps fill in any nutrient gaps that your regular meals may need to include.

Moreover, getting plenty of exercises—which boosts blood flow to the brain—can help reduce stress levels while providing vital energy, which is essential for optimal performance.

Eating the right mix of nutrients, exercising regularly, and getting plenty of rest can help keep your mind, body, and spirit in sync. Incorporating the right amount of protein, fats, carbs, and fiber into your meals helps ensure they are balanced while keeping your cholesterol levels and blood pressure within the normal range.

Regular exercise helps keep your heart healthy by increasing blood flow throughout the body and reducing stress levels. In contrast, adequate rest helps boost mental alertness. Taking care of your physical health is an important step towards looking after your overall well-being.

Take a Nap for Memory Enhancement

Are you looking for ways to improve your tennis serve? You may not realize it, but getting a good night's sleep is more beneficial than having a cup of coffee after your lesson. According to a study conducted by Sara Mednick, Ph.D., and her team at the University of California, San Diego, and supported by the NIMH, daytime naps are associated with improved motor learning, verbal memory, and all other types of learning related to tennis serving.

While approximately 90% of Americans consume caffeine daily, the stimulant effects of caffeine are short-lived. They should not be used as a substitute for sleep.

Research conducted by Mednick and her team has demonstrated that daytime naps, like nighttime sleep, can improve alertness and boost memory. Furthermore, their studies have revealed that taking a nap after learning something new enhances motor skills and verbal memory.

Read Books

It's important to remember that IQ is not fixed and can be increased through the right activities - one of these being education.

Research by the University of Edinburgh found that a year of exposure to academic content can increase an individual's IQ by five points! So, if you're looking for a way to boost your cognitive power, invest in yourself and take the time to learn something new.

Successful people today know that reading books is a habit that makes you smarter and wiser. By reading, you gain knowledge about things others may not be aware of, giving you a unique perspective on various subjects. So if you want to increase your brain power and earn the respect of others, start reading more books.

Shake Up Your Routine

Your brain needs to be challenged to grow and develop. Whenever you do something, your brain forms a neural pathway - and as you repeat the same action over time, that pathway becomes stronger.

If you always approach tasks the same way, your brain won't be pushed to create new pathways. To help break free from bad habits, it's important to switch up your routine and think of new ways of tackling problems: this will help your brain progress but can also help you break away from unhelpful habits.

Changing your habits can help you break free from bad behavior and kickstart your brain.

For example, if you've been reaching for a bottle of alcohol after a stressful day at work, it's important to switch up your routine. Instead of heading straight home, consider visiting a friend - make sure it will not encourage you to continue the same bad habits!

With this approach, you'll not only be able to break away from addiction. Still, you can also help improve your cognitive abilities.

Restrict Your Crossword Solving Time

To make it worse, research has shown that it does not offer much value in training the brain or preventing a disease like Alzheimer's. It doesn't mean you should stop playing it, especially if you find it fun.

Yet think that it's contributing little to your ability to solve practical problems. Crossword puzzles should be removed from that list if you want activities that can boost your decision-making and problem-solving ability because they offer little regarding these aspects.

While it can be tempting to rely on crossword puzzles to challenge our brains, recent studies have suggested that this isn't the case. It has been found that these activities can strain the brain rather than help to sharpen it - so relying on them may not necessarily make us smarter!

Taking a more active approach to tackling mental tasks and trying different strategies is more likely to lead to cognitive improvements.

Engage Your Audience

Unlocking the power of stories can be a wonderful way to sharpen your brain. Telling stories about past events can help solidify memories and effectively communicate moments with others.

If you want to try it out, make sure you avoid recounting traumatic events - instead, why not try making a joke out of it and show that you've moved on? Doing this can help boost your brain power and give you some much-needed relief from the great moments in life.

Electronics

Power down your electronics at least half an hour before you hit the hay to ensure you get more restful sleep. In the era of digital devices, it's becoming increasingly difficult to maintain a healthy lifestyle.

Excessive use of technology can lead to addiction, sleep problems, and even mental health issues like Fear of Missing Out (FOMO). Spending too much time on social media affects our physical well-being.

It can seriously impact our mental well-being by creating unnecessary stress and anxiety. We must practice self-control and limit our online time to protect ourselves from these side effects.

Spending too much time on digital devices like TVs and games can adversely impact our brain activities. Instead, why not focus your time and energy on physical exercise and connecting with friends and family?

Exercise helps improve your brain's ability to learn new skills, balance, and measure distance - all important things for having a healthy mental state. To ensure you get a deep, restful sleep every night, switch off your screens at least half an hour before bedtime.

Expand Your Knowledge!

Improving your skills can boost your brain power. For example, learning to play a new instrument helps you translate what you see into what you do. This process requires your brain to create several neural pathways, which is excellent for brain power. Similarly, learning a new language can also have a positive impact on your thinking and expression abilities.

Studies have found that learning dance can help seniors reduce their risk of Alzheimer's. When picking up a new skill, make sure you choose something you find interesting and useful so that it will be easy to stay motivated. Think carefully before deciding what to learn - the right skill can positively benefit your mental well-being.

CHAPTER 13

Enhanced Mental Health

You can enjoy several direct and indirect benefits by improving your brain health and power. A healthy brain's benefits include improved memory, increased focus, concentration, and enhanced critical thinking skills. A healthy brain can also lead to improved mental well-being and increased productivity.

Optimize Your Bodily Performance

Your brain is your body's powerhouse - it controls how you function, understands, and interpret the world around you. When it's working at its peak performance, it can positively affect every other part of your body.

From improved coordination and muscle performance to increased mental well-being and productivity, taking care of your brain health will pay off in many ways.

When you improve y, You can enjoy several direct and indirect benefits when you improve your brain health, including improved memory, increased focus concentration, and enhanced critical thinking skills. A healthy brain can also lead to improved mental well-being and increased productivity.

Clarity and Focus

Your brain greatly affects how alert and focused you are throughout the day. Neurochemicals, such as caffeine and Ginkgo biloba, can help improve or alter brain functions, improving your alertness and focus.

When your brain functions, it can positively affect every other part of your body - from improved coordination and muscle performance to increased mental well-being and productivity. Taking care of your brain health not only has immediate benefits but long-term ones as well.

Taking care of your brain health for the long term is important. Unhealthy habits can harm your brain, decreasing mental clarity, focus, and energy levels. Adopting healthy habits such as getting enough sleep, eating well, exercising regularly, and limiting stress can help keep your brain functioning at its highest level.

Incorporating supplements like Ginkgo biloba and caffeine into your lifestyle can provide additional benefits related to alertness and focus. Taking care of your brain health is essential for overall body wellness - both now and in the future.

Enhanced Efficiency

Taking care of your brain health is the best way to ensure that your cognitive performance remains at its peak and that you can still perform basic daily activities without difficulty.

There are simple things you can do to preserve your brain health and reduce age-related cognitive decline. Exercise, healthy eating habits, getting enough sleep, and supplements like Ginkgo biloba or caffeine are all effective ways to protect your brain health.

Stimulating mental activities such as crossword puzzles and Sudoku can help keep your mind sharp and active. Start making these lifestyle changes today and reap the benefits later in life.

Preserving your brain health is essential for living a long and healthy life. Not only will it help you to maintain a high level of intelligence, but it could also help you to stay independent into old age. Taking care of your brain health involves:

- Exercise.
- Eating healthy.
- Getting enough sleep.
- Taking supplements like Ginkgo biloba or caffeine.
- Engaging in stimulating mental activities such as crosswords and Sudoku.

Making these lifestyle changes now could prevent age-related cognitive decline later in life - ensuring that you keep your brain functioning at its best.

Exercise

Exercise can be incredibly powerful for keeping your brain in top condition.

Not only does exercise reduce the risk of physical health issues, but it can also improve memory and cognitive function. Studies have found that three times a week, just 30 minutes of moderate-intensity aerobic exercise was linked to improvements in mental performance.

Exercise increases blood flow to the brain, helps increase the production of hormones that improve concentration, and releases endorphins that positively affect mood. With regular exercise, you can keep your brain healthy and sharp well into old age.

Exercise doesn't have to be expensive or time-consuming. There are plenty of ways to incorporate physical activity into your daily routine.

Even a short walk, jog, or bike ride can help to increase your brain's oxygen levels and reduce stress. You can even do simple exercises at home without costly gym fees or equipment.

Regular exercise has been linked to increased focus and memory recall, improved sleep quality, and overall mental health. Make sure you're taking regular breaks from your workday for some physical activity - it will make a huge difference to your physical and mental health!

Soak Up Those Vitamin D Rays!

The benefits of sunlight are often overlooked, but Vitamin D, the happy hormone produced when exposed to UVB rays from the sun, plays a key role in the health of our brains.

Research has shown that adequate levels of Vitamin D can improve cognitive function, reduce depression and anxiety, and even help protect against memory decline. To ensure you're getting enough Vitamin D, try to find a daily balance between natural exposure to daylight and avoiding too much direct exposure to the sun's ultraviolet rays.

Doing so can ensure that your brain gets the Vitamin D it needs for optimal mental health.

While natural sunlight is the best source of Vitamin D, there may be times when you cannot get enough from the sun - especially during winter or if you live in a part of the world with less direct daylight.

In this case, it is advisable to take Vitamin D supplements as part of your daily routine. Be sure to consult your physician before doing so, and always take care not to take more than is recommended, as it can cause side effects. Ensure you get enough Vitamin D to help keep your brain healthy and functioning optimally!

Say Yes to Tetris

We often think of fun activities like video games as mere entertainment. Still, they can be surprisingly beneficial for the brain! For example, playing the classic Tetris game has increased grey matter in the brain. It helps to improve our spatial abilities, making us more efficient at tasks such as problem-solving and navigation.

Furthermore, playing Tetris after a traumatic experience has been found to help keep memories of that event from being stored in the mind too deeply. So put down your phone and pick up a controller - it's much more than just a pleasant distraction!

We often think of fun activities like video games as mere entertainment. Still, they can be surprisingly beneficial for the brain! For example, playing the classic game of Tetris has been shown to reduce the frequency of flashbacks to negative memories.

If you have a phone or tablet, try to install this game and play it during your leisure period - it might help you more than you realize!

Meditation

Meditation and mindfulness are becoming increasingly popular as people discover their importance. Not only can it help reduce stress, but studies have found that it can also help prevent age-related disorders like Alzheimer's or dementia. Just 15 minutes a day can significantly impact your life - try it, and you will immediately feel the effects!

Meditation has benefits far beyond what any supplement can provide. It can boost cognitive longevity, improve the immune system, reduce stress, and even help prevent depression. Take some time to meditate daily, and you'll find that your brain power, health, and overall well-being will improve!

Foster Lasting Relationships

In pursuing success, staying focused on your work without taking time to interact with others can be tempting. But this risks loneliness and isolation - particularly as freelancing and remote working become more popular.

It can have a detrimental effect on cognitive health, so it is important to make sure you connect with other people and build strong relationships.

Maintaining a balance between work and relationships is important for our cognitive health and overall well-being.

Feeling lonely or isolated can have serious consequences, including increased blood pressure, poorer quality of sleep, depression, and lowered well-being. To ensure that you avoid falling into this trap, make sure to stay connected with family and friends regularly.

Reduce Anxiety and Pressure

Eating for your brain is essential to staying healthy and maintaining a balanced lifestyle. To ensure optimal cognitive functioning, your diet must include antioxidants, amino acids, vitamin E, nuts, blueberries, whole grains, and avocados. Also, moderate consumption of wine is thought to improve cognitive function.

Taking care of your physical health is important, but eating for both body and mind will help you become healthier and more well-rounded.

It's impossible to avoid stress altogether in today's world, with the pressure to perform and be our best all around us. That being said, it's important to recognize when stress levels are becoming too high and utilize techniques to help you manage it before it affects your physical and cognitive functioning.

Stress management techniques such as yoga, mindfulness meditation, listening to music, journaling, or taking up a hobby can help reduce tension and promote relaxation.

CHAPTER 14

Nourish Your Mind with Nutritious Foods

Eating habits are an important part of our overall health and well-being. According to the World Health Organization, health is defined as "a state of complete physical, mental and social well-being," so maintaining healthy eating habits is a crucial step towards achieving this.

Scientific studies have shown that food affects physical, mental, emotional, and social health. So being mindful of what we eat is essential to maintain balance.

Eating for your brain is essential to staying healthy and maintaining a balanced lifestyle. To ensure optimal cognitive functioning, your diet must include antioxidants, amino acids, vitamin E, nuts, blueberries, whole grains, and avocados.

Also, moderate consumption of wine is thought to improve cognitive function. Taking care of your physical health is important, but eating for both body and mind will help you become healthier and more well-rounded.

Findings in a Study

In this study, 61 participants were tasked to learn verbal memory, motor, and perceptual tasks in the morning. After lunch, one group was given a nap of 60 to 90 minutes, while another two groups listened to audiobooks with either 200mg of caffeine (equivalent to a Tall Starbucks brewed coffee) or placebo pills, respectively.

In the afternoon, all three groups underwent tests to assess how much they had learned from the earlier tasks. The results revealed that napping greatly benefited all types of learning tested, while caffeine impaired motor learning and verbal memory.

The study revealed that the nap group outperformed the caffeine and placebo groups in recalling words and tasks of perceptual learning.

Even though the placebo group was not given any caffeine, their results were still better than those of the caffeine group. This could be attributed to a placebo effect, as participants may have believed they were given caffeinated pills.

The findings from this study demonstrate that napping in the afternoon can be beneficial for learning and memory, whereas caffeine may have an adverse effect.

Ginkgo

Ginkgo leaf extract has a long history of use in traditional Chinese medicine, with evidence pointing to its potential health benefits.

In modern times, people have been using ginkgo leaf extracts to help improve memory and cognitive functions and treat or prevent Alzheimer's disease and other types of dementia. Ginkgo extract is also used for intermittent claudication (leg pain caused by narrowing arteries), multiple sclerosis, tinnitus, sexual dysfunction, and other health conditions.

Ginkgo extracts are typically taken orally in tablets, capsules, or teas but can also occasionally be found in skin products.

Studies on the efficacy of ginkgo have yielded mixed results. Some studies have shown promise for ginkgo's effectiveness in treating intermittent claudication. Still, more research is needed to confirm these findings.

People who take anticoagulant drugs, have bleeding disorders, or are due to undergo surgery or dental procedures should use caution when taking ginkgo, as it may increase the risk of bleeding. It is important to speak with a healthcare professional before using ginkgo to weigh the potential risks and benefits carefully.

It is essential to inform your healthcare providers if you use complementary and alternative practices to manage your health. This will give them a better understanding of your full health picture, allowing for safe and coordinated care.

Ginkgo seeds contain ginkgo toxin, which can cause seizures and even death if consumed in large quantities over time. Ginkgo leaves and ginkgo leaf extract are considered much safer as they contain very little of this toxin.

The ginkgo leaf extract is the preferred form for its possible health benefits. Taking ginkgo should always be done with caution; it is important to adhere to dosage instructions and consult a healthcare professional before consuming any amount.

Blueberries

A recent USDA study found that a diet rich in the blueberry extract may enhance short-term memory in aging rats.

This exciting research could have major implications for humans, with Agriculture Secretary Dan Glickman noting, "If this finding holds for humans, it should further encourage consumption of fruits and vegetables high in antioxidants to help fight the effects of aging."

Researchers found that feeding extracts of blueberries, strawberries, or spinach to elderly rats daily for eight weeks improved their short-term memory. The blueberry extract also showed additional benefits, helping to improve the rat's balance and coordination. These findings have positive implications for maintaining cognitive function in humans as we age.

This exciting and potentially groundbreaking study shows how fruits and vegetables could prevent loss of function in aging and reverse dysfunctions in behavior and nerve cells. It is the first to demonstrate such results – and could have vast implications for improving cognitive health as we age.

Studies have indicated that blueberries, strawberries, and spinach are highly effective at subduing oxygen free radicals, compounds that can cause serious damage to cells, DNA, and other delicate internal components – leading to dysfunctions and diseases associated with aging. However, this new research suggests that the consumption of these fruits and vegetables may be able to reverse some of the issues caused by these radicals.

As backed by science, let's discover how to supercharge your brain using food and exercise. To help with that process, here are some tips on ways you can sharpen your cognitive abilities.

Drink Coffee

Coffee has become a morning ritual for many of us, and it's not just to satisfy our taste buds - coffee can also give your cognitive powers a short-term boost! It has this effect because it contains caffeine, which helps you stay alert and focused.

It can be especially helpful when undertaking tasks that require precision or are mundane and repetitive. So, the next time you need an extra jolt of energy for your work, why reach for your favorite cup of joe?

When you need to be extra alert or quick to react, having a substance that can boost your alertness can help you to be more productive with tasks that demand concentration. But remember - don't abuse this substance, as it's important not to develop an unhealthy dependency on it. Enjoy the benefits of caffeine in moderation and reap the rewards when you need them.

Fatty Fish

Fatty fish, such as salmon, trout, and sardines, are one of the best sources of omega-3 fatty acids that our brains need. Omega-3 fats make up roughly half of the fat content in our brains and play a crucial role in learning and memory. Eating fatty fish regularly can help keep your brain functioning at its peak and ensure overall health.

Green Tea

Green tea can have remarkable effects on brain function. It has been proven to improve alertness, memory, and performance and enhance focus.

It contains nutrients like L-theanine which can increase the activity of a neurotransmitter called GABA, making it an ideal beverage for those trying to boost their brain functions. So next time you need to pick me up, reach for green tea instead of coffee!

L-theanine is a special amino acid found in green tea that helps to reduce anxiety and puts you in a relaxed state. It does this by crossing the blood-brain barrier and increasing the frequency of alpha waves in the brain, resulting in relaxation without fatigue.

Research has indicated that it can be used to counteract the stimulating effects of caffeine! So, if you're looking for an effective way to de-stress, reach for a cup of green tea.

Oranges

Did you know that a single medium-sized orange can give you all the Vitamin C your body needs in one day? This essential nutrient has plenty of benefits for your brain health and helps prevent mental decline.

It may even protect against age-related declines and Alzheimer's disease. So, make sure to include Vitamin C-rich foods such as oranges in your diet for better brain health!

Vitamin C provides strong antioxidant protection against the damaging effects of free radicals on the brain and can also support overall brain health - especially as you age.

Fortunately, adding Vitamin C-rich foods such as oranges, guava, bell peppers, strawberries, tomatoes, and kiwi to your diet is an easy way to get the nutrient your brain needs. So, start filling up your plate with these goodies today!

Eggs

Eggs are a great source of essential Vitamins B12, B6, choline, and folate. Choline is especially important for producing acetylcholine - a neurotransmitter that plays an integral role in memory and blood regulation. Increasing choline intake could even help improve your memory and mental function. So go ahead and add some eggs to your plate today!

Many nutrients are important for brain health, and choline is one of the most critical. Unfortunately, many people don't get enough choline in their diet.

However, increasing your choline intake is easy - eat more eggs! Egg yolks are a great source of this nutrient. Additionally, Vitamin B plays several important roles in brain function. For example, they can help slow the aging process - especially in older adults. So, make sure to include eggs in your diet daily to support your brain health!

Nuts

Eating nuts can bring numerous benefits to your health, including improved markers of heart health. Additionally, research has shown that eating nuts may help to improve cognition and protect against neurological diseases.

Not only that but there is evidence to suggest that women who eat nuts regularly may have a better memory than those who don't. So, add some tasty and nutritious nuts to your diet today for a healthier brain!

Incorporating nuts into your diet is a great way to improve brain health. Nuts are full of important nutrients like healthy fats, Vitamin E, and antioxidants that all contribute to improved brain function.

Walnuts are particularly beneficial due to their high content of omega-3 fatty acids. Eating walnuts regularly can help protect the brain from free radical damage, slowing aging. So, start adding walnuts to your diet today for a healthier mind!

Dark Chocolate

Dark chocolate is more than a delicious treat - it's also good for your brain! Caffeine and antioxidants help keep alertness and focus. At the same time, flavonoids are known to positively affect learning, memory, and other cognitive processes. If you need a brain boost, why not try dark chocolate? Not only will you enjoy the taste, but you'll be giving your mind that extra push it needs!

Chocolate can boost your mental performance. Recent studies have indicated that dark chocolate flavonoids may help enhance memory and delay age-related mental decline.

Plus, a study involving 900 people showed that those who ate dark chocolate or cocoa regularly performed better on memory-related tasks. Lastly, it's also well known that dark chocolate can provide an immediate happiness boost due to its mood-boosting properties. So, make yourself feel good and improve your cognitive abilities by indulging in some yummy dark chocolate today!

Pumpkin Seeds

Pumpkin seeds are a nutritious snack that can boost your brain and body! Not only are they full of antioxidants to help protect against free radical damage, but pumpkin seeds are also high in essential minerals like iron, magnesium, copper, and zinc.

Of these, zinc is especially important for proper nerve functioning. Research indicates that a lack of zinc in the diet may lead to neurological issues such as Parkinson's disease, Alzheimer's disease, or depression, making pumpkin seeds even more valuable when taking care of your mental health! So why grab yourself a handful of pumpkin seeds today? You'll be doing your brain some serious good!

Did you know that certain minerals can greatly impact your mental health? Magnesium is essential for learning and memory, so its deficiency can result in epilepsy, migraines, or depression.

Copper helps control nerve signals, with low levels leading to neurological disorders like Alzheimer's. Iron is needed for blood production, and its deficiency has been linked to brain fog and impaired brain function.

Thankfully, there are several ways to increase your intake of these valuable minerals - from eating foods such as pumpkin seeds or dark chocolate to taking supplements - meaning you don't have to worry about the effects of being nutrient deficient anymore!

Broccoli

Broccoli is an incredibly nutritious vegetable, making it one of the top picks for dieticians everywhere. Its abundance of potent plant compounds and antioxidants makes it a great source of protection from free radical damage. But broccoli's health benefits do not end there!

Broccoli is also high in Vitamin K; 1 cup (91 gram) serving provides 100% of the Recommended Daily Intake (RDI). This fat-soluble vitamin plays an important role in brain cell formation and is vital for proper brain functioning.

If you're looking to bolster your mental health, adding some broccoli to your diet is the perfect way to do so!

Broccoli is one of those rare superfoods packed with multiple benefits for your brain. Studies have shown that Vitamin K can help improve memory, especially in older adults - and broccoli provides 100% of the recommended daily intake (RDI) of Vitamin K in just a single serving!

Broccoli also contains other compounds that can produce anti-inflammatory and antioxidant effects, protecting your brain from damage and promoting healthy aging. So, the next time you plan an all-brain diet, remember to add some delicious broccoli to that plate!

Turmeric

Turmeric is one of the most talked-about spices recently - and it is not hard to see why! It is a key ingredient found in curry powder. Its active ingredient, curcumin, has been scientifically proven to cross the blood-brain barrier, making it one of the few substances that can directly benefit brain cells.

Studies have shown that turmeric can help reduce inflammation, improve memory and cognitive function, encourage neurogenesis, and protect against oxidative damage. With all these benefits backed by science, adding some turmeric to your diet could be a great way to boost your brain health!

Turmeric is a powerful antioxidant and anti-inflammatory compound that drastically improves brain health. Besides promoting cognitive function and memory, its active ingredient, curcumin, can help clear amyloid plaques, a trademark of Alzheimer's disease.

It also helps improve mood by boosting feel-good hormones such as serotonin and dopamine. Research also suggests that turmeric can support neurogenesis, or the growth of new brain cells - making it an all-around brain booster!

Creatine

Creatine is a natural substance that plays a role in energy metabolism and can be found in small amounts in the brain. It's mostly found in muscles and food sources such as eggs, fish, and meat. Creatine is a popular supplement among vegetarians, as it provides a source of this nutrient they would otherwise be lacking.

Acetyl-L-Carnitine

Acetyl-L-carnitine (ALCAR) is an amino acid that the body produces naturally. It has a major role in energy metabolism. Research has shown that taking ALCAR supplements can make you more alert, slow down age-related memory loss, and improve memory. ALCAR is a popular supplement and can be easily found in most vitamin stores.

Animal studies have suggested that this supplement may help prevent age-related cognitive decline and improve learning. Human studies also suggest it could be effective in slowing the decline in cognitive function due to aging and improving cognitive function in people with Alzheimer's and mild dementia.

Resveratrol

Resveratrol is an antioxidant that occurs naturally in the skin of purple and red fruits such as raspberries, grapes, and blueberries. It's also served with chocolate, peanuts, and red wine. Research evidence shows that resveratrol consumption could prevent the deterioration of the hippocampus, an important part of the brain that plays a vital role in memory.

Moreover, resveratrol consumption could delay the decline in brain function that many people experience as they age. In a study involving a small group of healthy older adults, it was discovered that consuming 200 mg of this supplement daily for 26 weeks enhances memory. If you're interested in trying it, you can find this supplement in stores and online.

Phosphatidylserine

Phosphatidylserine is a kind of fat compound known as phospholipids and can be found in the brain. Taking this supplement can help preserve brain health, potentially reducing the age-related decline in brain function. A study showed that taking 100 mg of this supplement three times a day could lead to such benefits.

Moreover, research has shown that healthy people taking up to 400 mg of this supplement daily can experience improved thinking ability and memory. However, more studies are needed to better understand its effect on the brain. Luckily, this supplement is easy to find in both stores and online.

Folic Acid

According to various studies, vitamins B6, B12, and B9 are essential for overall brain health. Pregnant women and those low-consuming doses of these vitamins should consider supplementing, as they each play a crucial role in preventing congenital disabilities.

For those at high risk of developing Alzheimer's disease, doctors may recommend taking them - though there is still debate about their effectiveness in such cases. Without medical advice, getting enough leafy greens is usually a good place to start.

Ginseng

Ginseng is often combined with Ginkgo biloba and is popular among those seeking increased brain power, especially in Asia. While research has pointed to its mental benefits, some studies have yet to make the same observations.

More research is needed to understand t fully understand Ginseng's effects on cognitive performance hand, and anecdotal evidence suggests that it may improve memory and thinking functions, but due to an. Still, scientific caution should be exercised when considering this supplement for everyday use.

Combinations

Combining supplements may be beneficial for some, but since they are still chemical substances and can have serious side effects, it is never recommended to experiment with them.

Some people also claim that their medications become more effective when taken with supplements - though it's important to utilize medical advice and not make assumptions. Ultimately, it is always best to seek a doctor before starting any new supplement or drug regime.

While many supplements come from natural sources, it's important to remember that these substances and ingredients can still be dangerous when taken in the wrong combinations or with other drugs. That's why it's always best to seek medical advice before taking any combination of supplements or medications - as a wrong decision could have disastrous effects. Taking the time to consult an expert provides peace of mind. It ultimately ensures you don't regret any choices regarding your health.

CHAPTER 15

How Seniors can Preserve Brain Health

Aging is inevitable. No matter how meticulous you are with practicing healthy eating habits and regular exercise, you will still grow old. The best you can do is to slow down the process and ensure that you don't fall sick often during that period. This chapter will explore common brain dysfunctions associated with aging and how older adults can preserve their brain health and power.

Older people are not doomed to suffer from neurological dysfunction or illness. There are many steps they can take to preserve their brain health and power while they age.

Reconsidering Forgetfulness

We all have those fleeting moments where we can't remember why we're in a certain room or what we need. One day you forget where your car keys are, and the next time it's your reading glasses - such occurrences are commonplace.

Memory lapses are natural and can happen to anyone. However, when does memory loss become abnormal enough that it is necessary to consult a health expert? Here are some queries you should ask yourself: ·

Does memory loss disrupt daily living? According to John Hart, Jr., M.D., professor of behavioral and brain sciences at the University of Texas at Dallas and medical science director at the Center for Brain Health, if someone is having difficulty undertaking activities that were second nature before such as balancing a checkbook or keeping up with personal hygiene, it may be time to seek assistance.

Furthermore, driving should be monitored closely due to any potentially impaired judgment caused by memory problems.

How often do memory blunders happen? While it is common to occasionally forget where you parked your automobile, forgetting the same spot daily or scheduling meetings and then completely overlooking them is common. Regular memory lapses will likely be noticed since they disrupt your normal activities.

According to Hart, "It's normal to forget the name of someone you just met, but it may not be normal to permanently forget the name of a close friend or relative." Furthermore, "It also may not be normal never to remember meeting someone after you have spent a great deal of time with them."

It might indicate an issue if you have difficulty retaining entire conversations or details from those talks. Also, red flags that something could be wrong include frequently repeating yourself or asking the same questions numerous times in one conversation.

Do you recognize any signs of disorientation? If someone is experiencing extreme memory loss, they might become lost in a place they know well or even put items in peculiar places due to forgetfulness. For instance, placing car keys inside the refrigerator could indicate this issue.

If your memory loss is on a steady decline, it's important to have a healthcare provider evaluate it. Don't wait - if you're concerned that your waning recollection or forgetting more frequently could indicate something serious, seek professional help as soon as possible!

Factors Contributing to Memory Loss

Anything that influences cognition—how we think, learn, and remember—can affect memory.

Therefore, doctors often use an amalgamation of strategies to understand better what is happening. Physicians evaluate memory loss through a comprehensive approach, including obtaining the patient's medical history, evaluating mental functioning with questions, physical and neurological assessments, and blood or urine testing.

Computerized axial tomography (CAT) scans or magnetic resonance imaging (MRI) provide valuable information to identify any strokes and tumors that could result in memory issues. All these techniques should be applied to rule out reversible causes of memory loss and detect if it is due to a more serious brain disease.

Memory loss can have numerous causes, some of which may occur in combination. Here are a few potential contributors:

Numerous medications can interfere with memory, such as sleeping pills and antihistamines bought over the counter or via prescription. Some antidepressants and medications used to treat schizophrenia may also affect memory recall. Pain medicines employed after surgery are another group of pharmaceuticals that could affect your ability to remember things.

The excessive consumption of alcohol can deplete the body's essential Vitamin B1 (thiamine), resulting in impaired memory. In addition, alcohol and illegal drugs may alter brain chemicals linked to the cognitive recall.

Stress, particularly due to psychological trauma, can be debilitating and cause memory loss. Extreme cases of stress may even lead to psychogenic amnesia - a condition where one cannot remember their name, date of birth, or other key information; however, this will usually resolve on its own over time!

Depression is a common problem among the elderly and can lead to difficulty focusing, attention, and memory. Fortunately, treating depression often improves mood and resolves many associated memory issues.

A traumatic head injury can leave a person feeling disoriented, with potential difficulty in recalling memories. Fortunately, the memory loss associated with such an event is usually stable or improves over time; it rarely worsens.

People suffering from destructive infections such as HIV, tuberculosis, syphilis, herpes, and other diseases affecting the brain's lining or substance may be more prone to memory issues.·

Impaired thyroid functioning - hyperthyroidism or hypothyroidism – can adversely affect one's recall of recent happenings.

Your memory can be adversely impacted when you don't receive the optimal rest due to anxiety, insomnia, or sleep apnea. Sleep deprivation is a serious issue that should not be overlooked.·

Memory loss is often a result of vitamin B1 and B12 deficiencies. Fortunately, these can be easily treated with either an injection or an oral supplement.

As we all age, it can become more difficult to remember certain details, such as people's names. This is a natural part of the aging process and nothing to be alarmed about.

Do you often need help remembering details? Do these difficulties not drastically limit your daily life? You may be experiencing Mild Cognitive Impairment (MCI). An unusually impaired memory recognizes this condition compared to others of the same age. Yet, it does not hinder everyday activities like work or school.

Mild Cognitive Impairment

When someone has Mild Cognitive Impairment (MCI), they experience memory deficits while still performing daily activities without meeting the diagnosis requirements for dementia.

With age-related, ordinary forgetfulness, one may be unable to remember a name; in contrast, MCI produces more serious and prolonged memory impairments. MCI presents as an intermediary stage between normal aging and the more severe issues caused by Alzheimer's Disease. However, it is important to note that not all individuals with MCI will decline; studies suggest that roughly 12-15% per year of those affected progress into AD.

Scientists are currently investigating if the medications established to treat Alzheimer's symptoms may potentially benefit people with Mild Cognitive Impairment. Their aspiration is that, through accurate and timely evaluation and treatment of individuals suffering from MCI in the future, further degeneration can be deterred.

Neurological Dysfunctions

Many diseases and dysfunctions are associated with aging. Some of these dysfunctions affect brain health and brain power, reducing the efficiency of brain functioning.

What Is Mild Forgetfulness?

Fortunately, there are several techniques that one can use to stay sharp and keep their mind alert, such as finding a hobby, spending time with friends, eating well, and exercising regularly.

Here are some tips for improving your memory:

- Learn a new skill.
- Volunteer in your community, school, or place of worship
- Spend time with friends and family whenever possible.
- Use memory tools such as big calendars, to-do lists, and notes to yourself.
- Put your wallet, purse, keys, and glasses in the same place daily.
- Get lots of rest.
- Exercise and eat well.
- Only drink a little alcohol.
- Get help if you feel depressed for weeks at a time.

What Is a Severe Memory Problem?

When it comes to memory problems, there is a difference between mild forgetfulness and severe memory problems.

While mild forgetfulness is common in aging, severe memory problems can be indicative of a serious condition such as dementia or Alzheimer's Disease. Signs of severe memory loss include difficulty paying bills, using the toilet, and managing personal safety. If you are experiencing any of these issues, it is important to seek medical help immediately.

Here are some signs of severe memory loss:

- Asking the same questions repeatedly
- Becoming lost in places you know well.
- I need to be able to follow directions.
- Getting very confused about time, people, and places
- You are not taking care of yourself—eating poorly, not bathing, or being unsafe.
- Getting lost in a place you know well may signify a serious memory problem.

· Having trouble with your memory may affect your driving.

When to See a Doctor

You must talk to your doctor immediately if you have a severe memory problem. There are several medical causes of memory problems that can be treated, such as:

· Some medications may cause memory loss, and if this is the case, changing medications may help.
· Feeling very sad and worried can also lead to serious memory problems. Treatment for such conditions may involve therapy or medication.

It is best to consult your doctor if you have an issue with your memory that requires further attention.

Medical Conditions

Certain medical conditions can cause serious memory problems, including:

· Bad reaction to certain medicines
· Depression
· Dehydration
· Not eating sufficient healthy foods or needing more vitamins and minerals.
· Minor head injuries
· Thyroid problems

These types of memory issues should go away once these conditions are treated. It is important to talk to your doctor if you believe any of these may be contributing to your memory loss.

Emotional Problems

Emotional problems can cause serious memory problems in older people. Feelings of sadness, loneliness, worry, and boredom can lead to confusion and forgetfulness.

It is important to stay active, spend time with family and friends, and learn new skills to combat these emotional issues. If necessary, you may need to see a doctor or counselor for treatment. Once help is received, your memory problems should improve.

Alzheimer's Disease

Affecting over 5 million Americans, Alzheimer's Disease (AD) is the most widespread form of dementia in individuals aged 65 and beyond. AD is a debilitating, progressing neurodegenerative disorder that manifests through abnormal protein deposits (amyloid plaques) and nerve cell fiber tangles within the brain.

Age and family history are two big risk factors for developing this condition; likewise, having experienced severe head trauma increases one's susceptibility to such an ailment.

AD slowly destroys a person's memory and capacity to learn, reason, make decisions, communicate, and complete day-to-day tasks. Memory loss progresses rapidly and includes disorientation, confusion, and an inability to remember recent events. Those with mild to moderate AD may be able to recall past events.

Still, they can become easily lost in familiar places. People with AD may experience changes in personality and behavior, such as isolation or mistrust. As the disease progresses, they lose their ability to speak and move normally until incapacitation and death occur. Here are some facts about treatment options for Alzheimer's Disease:

Most clinical studies investigating drug therapies to alleviate memory loss are conducted on those suffering from Alzheimer's disease. · Although there is no cure-all for Alzheimer's Disease, the FDA has approved five drugs to tackle its specific symptoms.

Four drugs, known as cholinesterase inhibitors, are believed to work similarly. Cognex (tacrine), Exelon (rivastigmine), and Raza dyne (galantamine) are approved for the treatment of mild to moderate AD. Aricept (donepezil) is approved for treating all degrees of severity, from mild to severe.

Cholinesterase inhibitors stop the breakdown of acetylcholine, a chemical used by nerves to communicate with each other. According to Susan Molchan, M.D., program director for the Alzheimer's Disease Neuroimaging Initiative project at the National Institute on Aging (NIA) - part of the National Institutes of Health - this type of drug may help delay or reduce symptoms in some people.

Possible side effects of cholinesterase inhibitors include nausea and diarrhea.

Namenda (memantine) is approved for moderate to severe AD and works by blocking the action of glutamate. This chemical may be overactive in people with AD. It may help some patients maintain certain daily activities for longer periods.

Common side effects include dizziness, headaches, constipation, and confusion. Namenda is often prescribed with a cholinesterase inhibitor.

Symptoms of AD that pertain to behavior may include agitation, sleeplessness, anxiety, and depression. These symptoms can be treated.

Inhibiting and decreasing amyloid is a major focus of research due to its association with nerve cell death and being a component of the plaques that form in the brains of people with AD.

Secretase inhibitors are being developed and tested to block beta-amyloid production. At the same time, immunotherapy against beta-amyloid is also being studied with the possibility that it could help reduce amyloid deposits.

Clinical trials are underway to test the effects of secretase inhibitors on people with Alzheimer's. So far, results have been mixed, with some trials showing improvement in symptoms and others not. More research is needed to determine if these drugs are effective and safe.

Recently published results from clinical trials involving secretase inhibitors for AD have been varied. In 2020, a trial to test the effects of verubecestat (a secretase inhibitor) on people with mild to moderate Alzheimer's disease showed no significant improvement in cognitive function or symptoms.

Another study published in 2018 found that patients treated with BACE1 inhibitors had reduced levels of beta-amyloid and improved cognitive outcomes. Further studies are needed to evaluate these drugs' effectiveness in treating Alzheimer's.

The 2018 study involving BACE1 inhibitors found that those treated with the drug exhibited reduced levels of beta-amyloid in their blood. This was accompanied by improved cognitive function and other symptoms related to Alzheimer's disease. However, the results of this trial were preliminary, and it is uncertain if these effects will be sustained over time.

Many other potential treatments for Alzheimer's disease are being studied. Some of these include -Cholinesterase inhibitors: These drugs increase the levels of acetylcholine in the brain, which is thought to help with memory and cognitive function. –

Anti-amyloid antibodies: These drugs target the beta-amyloid protein found in the brains of those with Alzheimer's disease. By clearing this protein from the brain, cognitive function may improve. -NMDA receptor antagonists:

These drugs block the NMDA receptor, which is involved in learning and memory. By doing so, cognitive function may improve. -Memantine: This drug limits the activity of glutamate, a chemical messenger in the brain that is thought to be involved in Alzheimer's disease. By limiting its activity, cognitive function may improve.

There are many other potential causes of dementia besides Alzheimer's diseases.

Multi-infarct Dementia

Multi-infarct Dementia is a medical condition that causes serious memory problems, but it is often unknown or undiagnosed. Unlike Alzheimer's, signs of multi-infarct dementia can happen suddenly as memory loss and confusion are caused by small strokes or changes in the blood supply to the brain.

If the strokes stop, you may remain stable for a long time and even get better. If, however, more strokes occur, your condition may worsen. To reduce your chances of getting this illness, taking care of high blood pressure is key. Talk to your doctor about treatments if you are concerned about multi-infarct dementia.

Lewy Body Dementia

This type of dementia is characterized by Lewy bodies, which are abnormal deposits of a protein called alpha-synuclein in the brain. Lewy body dementia can cause various symptoms, including mood, behavior, and cognition changes.

It affects multiple areas of the brain, causing cognitive decline, changes in alertness and attention, recurrent visual hallucinations, and motor problems like those seen with Parkinson's disease, such as rigidity. Treatment options are available to help manage the symptoms of this disorder. While antipsychotic medications can treat hallucinations, extreme caution should be taken because they may worsen them.

Frontotemporal Dementia

This form of dementia is caused by damage to the frontal and temporal lobes of the brain, which can lead to changes in personality and behavior, as well as difficulties with language and cognition. This type of dementia associated with the shrinking of the frontal and temporal anterior lobes of the brain.

Symptoms can include impulsive or listless behavior, socially inappropriate behavior, and progressive loss of language functions. Although there is no cure for frontotemporal dementia, antidepressants and behavior modification may help improve some symptoms.

Vascular dementia

This is a type of dementia caused by problems with the blood vessels in the brain. This can lead to a decrease in blood flow to the brain, which can cause symptoms such as memory loss, difficulty thinking, and changes in mood and behavior.

Treatment focuses on preventing future problems with the blood vessels by controlling risk factors such as smoking, diabetes, and high blood pressure.

Creutzfeldt-Jakob Disease (CJD)

It is a rare, degenerative brain disorder that can cause failing memory, behavioral changes, lack of coordination, and visual disturbances in the early stages. Mental impairment quickly becomes more severe as the illness progresses. There is no drug to cure or control CJD, but some drugs may help with symptoms.

Myopathy

A certain disorder of the brain can lead to muscle weakness known for its severity in the upper arms and thighs. It occurs when there is miscommunication between different parts of the brain, causing the muscles not to be able to function properly. Even though natural supplements may be used as treatment, it is best to consult a doctor before using them, as they can interact with other drugs or substances in potentially harmful ways.

Treatment for the condition requiring muscle weakness typically involves medications that can affect how messages are sent and received in the brain. These can range from antidepressants to various anticonvulsant drugs, muscle relaxants, or tubocurarine antagonists.

Before taking any combination of medications and supplements, you must speak with a medical professional to ensure you take the right action.

Though drugs are the primary course of treatment for muscle weakness, there may be natural remedies that can help reduce the symptoms. Supplements such as zinc, magnesium, or omega-3s have been known to help with muscle weakness and pain.

Herbal remedies like turmeric and ginger can also reduce inflammation and improve blood circulation. However, it is important to consult with a doctor before using any of these supplements or herbs, as they can potentially interact with other medications or substances in harmful ways.

Parkinson's Disease

Parkinson's disease is a chronic and progressive movement disorder that can devastate those suffering. It leads to malfunction and death of vital nerve cells in the brain, which can cause a person to become unable to live without support or assistance from family or friends. Medication can provide relief when available.

However, when all other options are exhausted, doctors may recommend surgery for such individuals. While the thought of undergoing surgery might be daunting, some Parkinson's patients have reported that it has helped them improve their quality of life by providing better control over their movements and decreasing motor symptoms.

Parkinson's disease is a chronic and progressive neurological disorder that affects movement. This disorder is caused by the death of nerve cells in the brain, resulting in a decrease in dopamine production.

As a result, those affected may experience a wide range of symptoms such as tremors, rigidity, slow movement, and difficulty with coordination and balance. Other physical effects include difficulties with speaking and swallowing, depression, fatigue, and memory loss. Additionally, Parkinson's can affect mental processes and emotions, leading to cognitive impairment or changes in behavior.

Parkinson's disease is a life-threatening medical condition affecting millions of people worldwide. It is caused by an interruption in the blood supply to part of the brain resulting in symptoms such as arm weakness, faces drooping and speech difficulty.

The treatments available can help manage these symptoms and improve quality of life, but they cannot cure the condition. It is a difficult journey for those dealing with this disease. Still, with proper care and support, it is possible to live a full and healthy life despite Parkinson's.

Stroke

One of the most common health concerns for seniors is stroke. A stroke occurs when the blood supply to the brain is cut off and can cause memory loss and other cognitive difficulties.

While treatments are available to help manage these symptoms, there is no known cure for stroke. However, some steps can be taken to prevent stroke, such as eating a healthy diet, exercising regularly, and maintaining a healthy weight.

Eating a healthy diet is one of the most effective ways to prevent stroke. To stick with this lifestyle, incorporate more fruit and vegetables into your diet – aim for at least five servings per day. Cut down on processed foods, takeaways, and snacks, often high in saturated fats, unhealthy sugars, and unnecessary calories.

Choose lean proteins such as chicken or fish to boost your heart health, and include healthy fats in your diet from sources such as avocado, nuts, seeds, and oily fish. Include plenty of whole grains and legumes, which provide essential vitamins, minerals, and fiber.

Remember to stay hydrated by drinking plenty of water every day and exercising regularly – even a short walk every day can help reduce stroke risk factors such as high blood pressure and elevated cholesterol levels. Lastly, taking steps to manage stress levels – relaxation techniques such as yoga or mindfulness can be helpful here too!

Eating a healthy diet is one of the most effective ways to prevent stroke. Here is a list of foods that can help:

- Leafy green vegetables like kale and spinach
- Blueberries, raspberries, and other berries
- Nuts such as almonds and walnuts.
- Avocados and olive oil
- Whole grains such as oats, quinoa, buckwheat, barley, and brown rice
- Beans, lentils, and chickpeas
- Omega-3-rich fish such as salmon, sardines, and mackerel
- Tofu or tempeh
- Flaxseeds

Amyotrophic Lateral Sclerosis (ALS)

ALS is a progressive disease that affects motor neurons, leading to the deterioration of the body's muscles. There is no known cure, but there are steps that can be taken to prevent it.

ALS is a progressive neurodegenerative disease that affects nerve cells in the brain and the spinal cord. The cause of ALS is still unknown, but contributing factors may include genetics, lifestyle choices, and environmental factors.

There is currently no cure for ALS, but treatments are available to help ease symptoms and slow the progression of the disease. The most common symptoms of ALS are muscle weakness, twitching muscles, slurred speech, difficulty swallowing, and shortness of breath.

As the disease progresses, these symptoms become more pronounced, leading to complete paralysis and death. ALS typically progresses slowly over several years, although some cases can progress rapidly over just a few months.

There is no one-size-fits-all treatment for ALS, but various treatments are available to help ease symptoms and prolong life. These include physical therapy, occupational therapy, speech therapy, medications to relieve muscle cramps and spasms, and respiratory assistance.

Patients may also require a feeding tube or ventilator to help with eating and breathing. Although there is currently no cure for ALS, research into potential treatments is ongoing. Clinical trials are currently underway testing new medications and other therapies to find a way to stop or reverse the progression of ALS.

Here are some steps to help prevent ALS:

1. Lead a healthy lifestyle - eating nutritious foods, exercising regularly, avoiding smoking, and drinking alcohol in moderation.
2. Get regular check-ups - annually seeing your doctor can help identify any potential signs or symptoms of the disease before it progresses too far.
3. Participate in clinical trials - research on ALS is still in its infancy, so there may be opportunities to join clinical trials researching new treatments or preventive measures.
4. Ensure all vaccinations are up to date - certain diseases, such as the flu, can worsen ALS if contracted by someone who already has the condition. Keeping current with vaccinations can help protect against this eventuality.
5. Manage stress and anxiety levels - relaxation techniques such as yoga or mindfulness can help maintain mental well-being and reduce the chances of developing ALS over time.

Myasthenia Gravis

Myasthenia gravis is a chronic autoimmune disorder that affects the transmission of signals from the brain to the muscles. This blockage in communication results in weakened muscles and fatigue, particularly after periods of rest.

This can severely impair a person's ability to perform everyday tasks such as walking or eating. Myasthenia gravis can also have several other symptoms, such as double vision, trouble swallowing, drooping eyelids, and difficulty speaking.

Thankfully, this disease is not fatal and can be managed with medication and lifestyle changes. In some cases, surgery may be needed to remove specific antibodies causing the nerve-muscle blockade. While there is no cure for myasthenia gravis, research continues into treatments that could improve the quality of life for those with this chronic condition.

Muscular Dystrophy

Spinal muscular atrophy (SMA) is a group of genetic, progressive muscle disorders caused by a defect in the survival motor neuron one gene. It affects the muscles closest to the body's trunk, causing them to weaken and eventually break down.

Symptoms of SMA can include difficulty breathing, pain, and muscle contractures that limit mobility and cause severe deformity. In severe cases, children may be unable to move or hold their heads up. At the same time, adults may experience muscle wasting and paralysis.

Since SMA is a genetic disorder, it cannot be cured. Still, treatments are available to help slow its progression and alleviate symptoms for those living with it. These treatments include physical therapy, occupational therapy, speech therapy, medications to relieve muscle cramps and spasms, and respiratory assistance.

Neuropathy

Peripheral Neuropathy is a disorder of the peripheral nerves that leads to weakness and numbness in the hands and feet.

This can be caused by systemic diseases such as diabetes or adverse medication reactions.

People with this condition often have difficulty performing everyday activities due to weakened muscles and impaired sensation. In addition to this physical disability, peripheral Neuropathy can cause mental health issues such as depression, anxiety, and insomnia.

Management can involve lifestyle changes such as eating a healthy diet, exercising regularly, and avoiding common nerve pain triggers. Medications may also be prescribed to reduce pain levels and improve the quality of life for those affected by this condition.

Stopping Forgetfulness?

Research has shown that a combination of estrogen and progesterone can increase the risk of dementia in women over 65. While clinical trials are underway to test specific interventions for prevention, there are some steps recommended by animal and observational studies that may help reduce the risk of memory problems.

These steps include eating a balanced diet with plenty of fruits and vegetables, exercising regularly, staying socially active, maintaining good sleep habits, reducing stress levels, avoiding alcohol and smoking, and engaging in activities that stimulate cognitive functioning, such as puzzles and games.

Recent research has shown that vascular diseases, such as heart disease and stroke, may be tied to the emergence of Alzheimer's Disease (AD), its intensity level, or even multi-infarct dementia. Therefore, keeping cholesterol levels low and controlling blood pressure is important for reducing one's risk of cognitive decline due to these conditions.

To maintain your cognitive functioning, avoid smoking and overindulging in alcohol. Research conducted by Harvard Medical School revealed that smokers performed far worse than non-smokers regarding memory tests. Excessive consumption of alcohol can also lead to a decline in memory recall capabilities.·

Eating a balanced diet can be an excellent way to preserve healthy cognitive functioning. According to a study published in Neurology, green leafy vegetables have the highest association with slowing down mental decline as people age.

Moreover, reducing foods high in saturated fat and cholesterol and including fish such as salmon and tuna, which contain beneficial omega-3 fatty acids in your diet, may help protect brain health!

Establish social connections to create a sense of well-being and lower your risk for dementia. A study published in the February 2007 edition of Archives of General Psychiatry concluded that loneliness increases one's vulnerability to dementia later in life.

Thus, staying socially connected can help reduce stress levels while protecting against age-related cognitive decline.·

Significantly improves your cognitive health by engaging in activities that require mental stimulation.

Researchers have suggested that participating in activities such as reading, writing, learning a new skill, playing games, and gardening can encourage the growth of brain cells and connections between them - all leading to potentially decreased risks of developing dementia. You can have a great memory if you put in the work. Let us show you the way and act today.

Engage Your Brain

As we age, we must focus on physical exercise and engage in activities that challenge the brain. Mustafa Husain, director of the geriatric psychiatry division at Duke University School of Medicine, believes mental exercises are just as important as physical exercises.

Playing cards, joining book clubs, watching sports games with friends, or using brain-training apps can help keep our brains sharp and active. Regularly engaging in mental exercise is an effective way to reduce memory loss and improve cognitive health.

Nurture Your Social Bonds

Staying connected socially is important to keeping the mind sharp and healthy as we age. When children leave home and parents are left alone, they may feel isolated and lonely.

However, social interactions positively affect mood and help keep depression at bay. Building relationships with family, friends, and even new acquaintances can help fight memory loss and maintain mental function.

Regular Medical Check-Ups

Be sure to visit the hospital before you're sick - regular check-ups can help you detect any potential issues early and give you the best chance of recovery.

Brain problems, vitamin deficiencies, diabetes, and thyroid disease, are all conditions that can affect your memory if left untreated - so protect yourself by ensuring you keep up with routine appointments at the doctor.

Vaccines and health screenings are an important part of staying proactive about your health – make sure you know what is recommended for you and keep up with any recommended tests or treatments to protect yourself from potential health risks now and in the future.

Being Proactive

Taking proactive steps to protect your health is one of the best things you can do for yourself. Maintaining a healthy diet, exercising regularly, getting enough rest, and avoiding dangerous behaviors can all help prevent unnecessary health risks. You should also ensure that you are up to date on recommended vaccines and screenings to detect any potential issues early so they can be treated properly.

How Family Members Can Help

Family members and friends can provide a major source of support for living with memory issues. They can help you exercise, socialize, and keep up your daily routines, reminding you of the time of day, where you live, and what is happening worldwide. Additionally, they can provide practical help such as:

- List of plans for each day.
- Notes about safety in the home.
- Written directions for using common household items.
- Make sure you know the difference between normal forgetfulness and potential signs of a more serious illness.
- Resources on how to cope with serious memory problems.

Resources

Various resources are available if you are looking for more information about memory loss. You can contact organizations such as Alzheimer's Society and Dementia UK for support groups, services, publications on Alzheimer's disease, research centers, and studies. Additionally, websites such as the National Institute on Aging's Alzheimer's Disease Education & Referral Center provide helpful info on the different types of dementia and its associated risk factors.

Alzheimer's Association

The Alzheimer's Association is a nonprofit organization that provides information and support for individuals with Alzheimer's disease and their families.

You can call the Alzheimer's Association to find out about local resources available in your area. They offer services ranging from caregiving and financial planning information to educational programs and support groups.

Alzheimer's Disease Education and Referral (ADEAR) Center

The Alzheimer's Disease Education and Referral (ADEAR) Center provides a wealth of information on Alzheimer's disease and related dementias. ADEAR is located at PO Box 8250, Silver Spring, MD 20907-8250, and you can reach them by phone at 1-800-438-4380 or visit their website for more information.

Eldercare Locator

Do you need information or assistance locating community resources such as home care, adult day care, and nursing homes? The Eldercare Locator is a service of the Administration on Aging funded by the Federal Government that can help you find what you are looking for in your area. You can reach them by phone at 1-800-677-1116.

CONCLUSION

Boosting Brain Health

We all know the brain is responsible for many aspects of our lives, but how can you boost your brain health?

From coffee to reducing dizziness when feeling alert to understanding that delusional images may result from a malfunctioning brain, there are many insights we can gain from this journey. Keeping your brain healthy should be a priority since it determines your mindset and overall life experience.

Enhance Quality of Life

It is important to your physical and mental health to leverage the tips you have learned in this book to boost brain health and enhance your quality of life.

Luckily, changes do not need to involve spending large amounts of money or buying supplements. Instead, taking advantage of this unique opportunity can give you the tools you need to make the rest of your life the best. Take it!

Share Your Feedback

I hope this letter finds you well! I wanted to take a moment to express my gratitude that you've taken the time to read my book. Thank you so much for buying it and investing your time and energy into engaging with its content and stories.

As an author, I pour my heart and soul into every book I write. I hope you found "Memory Improvement" entertaining, thought-provoking, and engaging. If my writing has inspired or moved you, I would be incredibly grateful if you could take a few moments to leave a review on Amazon.

As you might know, online reviews are incredibly important to authors like me. They help us reach a wider audience and provide valuable feedback that we can use to improve our writing in the future. That's why I humbly request that you consider rating "Memory Improvement" with a 5-star review.

By doing so, you'll be helping to support my work and allowing others to discover my book. Moreover, it would mean the world to me to know that you enjoyed my writing enough to recommend it to others.

Once again, thank you so much for choosing to read my book. Your support and encouragement mean everything to me. And if you have any questions or comments, please do not hesitate to reach out.

Warmly,

Trevor Ponder

Free Video Training Course

Learn from high-performing business leaders and achieve your goals with this FREE video training & PDF. Discover how to achieve balance, use your energy in the right direction, set realistic deadlines, and avoid burnout. Claim your free video training now at IQSelf.com.

- Discover strategies and tactics used by high-performing business leaders
- Learn how to achieve balance and manage all areas of your life
- Avoid burnout and prevent work from taking priority over enjoyment
- Use your energy in the right direction to achieve your goals
- Set realistic deadlines to increase your chances of success
- Avoid getting stuck by feeling and moving through your emotions quickly
- Choose to take action, even in tough moments, to create momentum
- Learn why being goal-oriented up to a point is good but can also turn negative
- Understand the importance of limiting your obsession with achieving your goals
- Say goodbye to repeatedly regurgitating facts and stories, which can harm your well-being.

Go to IQSelf.com now to claim your free video training.

About the Author

Hey there, memory mavens! I'm Trevor Ponder, the memory mastermind behind "Harness the Power of Memory Training for Greater Success."

But I'm more than just a master of memory - I'm also a bona fide brainiac and junkie passionate about helping people improve their memory and achieve their dreams.

You might be wondering how I became so obsessed with memory training. Well, let me tell you - it all started in college. I was one of those forgetful students who kept forgetting everything from my locker combination to my name (true story!). It was frustrating. But instead of wallowing in my mental mush, I decided to take action.

I started delving into the world of memory training, scouring books and websites for tips and tricks to help me remember better. And boy, did I strike gold. I found a treasure trove of techniques that would make Sherlock Holmes proud. From mnemonics to memory palaces, I discovered a whole new world of brain-boosting strategies that I couldn't wait to put to the test.

Before long, I was not only remembering my locker combination and my name, but also all sorts of other information that had eluded me in the past. I was hooked on memory training and its incredible power to transform my life.

And that's why I'm on a mission to share those brain-boosting strategies with the world. I want to help people overcome their forgetfulness and unlock their brains' full potential.

Subscribe to my newsletter:
✉ https://iqself.com

Made in the USA
Middletown, DE
17 September 2024

60497190R00102